Island Ebb & Flow

A Pioneer's Journal

Of Life

On Waldron Island

by
Frances K. Lovering

SECOND EDITION

Illumina
PUBLISHING

Island Ebb & Flow

Illumina Publishing
P.O. Box 2643, Friday Harbor, WA 98250
www.illuminapublishing.com

Second Edition, 2008
First Edition, First Printing 1985

Book cover and interior design
by Mitzi Johnson, Mitzi, Ltd.
Typestyle set in Goudy Oldstyle
Printed in the U.S.A. on recycled paper

Library of Congress Control Number: 2008936889

ISBN 978-0-9818092-3-6

Original Dedication
In loving memory of my husband, Captain Jim, and to our family,
Fran, Bill, and the grandchildren, Cindy, Matthew, Marty,
and Mitchell. To these dear people I dedicate this book
and my own personal part of Waldron.

Re-Dedication
I would like to dedicate this Second Edition to my late mother,
father and husband, Bill, as well as to my grandchildren:
Marty, Crysta, Curtis, Brittany, Brady, Sean and Lucas.
May they continue their own special memories of Waldron.
— *Fran Chevalier*

Publisher's Note

The family of Frances Lovering would like to continue to share her story for future generations to enjoy. This all came about through the dedication of daughter-in-law, Theresa Chevalier.

Originally published in 1985 in honor of Mrs. Lovering's 80th birthday, it was left as she saw it and wrote it, thus preserving the flavor and voice of this remarkable woman.

Acknowledgment

I would like to express my sincere thanks to Jim's brother, Phil, for his generous support during our early years on Waldron and for providing me with letters that were such a help in jogging the memory.

To my dear friend Violet Gray who sat patiently and listened, giving me constant encouragement, never doubting that my writing would reach fruition.

To Bob Major, editor at the University of Washington, who spurred me on and assured me of the potential of my early manuscript and for setting up guidelines in the use of "which" and "that."

To my friend, Donna Gallant, for her labor of love in typing the first rough drafts.

To Dr. Charles Ludwig who so generously gave me free rein and permission to use data from his writing of *A Brief History of Waldron*.

My thanks and appreciation to Bob Shaller who guided me over the rough spots with authority and gentle persuasion.

And to Dave Richardson, author of *The Pig War Islands*, for his tireless endeavor to catch the interest of publishers during a time of such poor economy.

To all of these concerned contributors I offer my heartfelt thanks. May God bless you all.

Those Days Past

Prologue	**Thinking Back**	IX
Chapter One	**Meet The Mate** *1933-1934*	1
Chapter Two	**Roots And Shoots**	13
Chapter Three	**Early Homesteading** *1860's-1932*	19
Chapter Four	**The Chicken Comes First** *1933-1934*	27
Chapter Five	**The Quarry Boom** *Early 1900's*	37
Chapter Six	**Growing Pains** *1935-1939*	43
Chapter Seven	**There's Eggs** *1940-1941*	61
Chapter Eight	**Meet The Master** *1942-1949*	65
Chapter Nine	**The Changing Tide** *1949*	67
Chapter Ten	**Waldron Cauldron** *1950-1954*	73

Chapter Eleven   **Old-time Bachelors**   91

Chapter Twelve   **Troubled Water**   97
1956-1957

Chapter Thirteen   **Ebb And Flow**   105
1958-1959

Chapter Fourteen   **The Waldron Word**   113
1958-1960

Chapter Fifteen   **"10-4, This Is Waldron"**   125
1961-1962

Chapter Sixteen   **Flood Tide**   143
1963-1964

Chapter Seventeen   **The Mail Flies Through**   157
1965-1966

Chapter Eighteen   **Cross Currents**   177
1966-1967

Chapter Nineteen   **Ebbing Tides**   189
1968-1970

Chapter Twenty   **Going Ashore**   207
1971-1976

Epilogue   **This Is My Song**   209

ISLAND EBB & FLOW · IX

Prologue
Thinking Back

Thinking back on Waldron Island the images rush forth unchecked: lilac, madrona, dogwood, apple and cherry blossoms all competing for my attention; the walks we would take along Waldron's sun-dappled roads when the pale new growth was on the fir, hemlock and pine; stumbling upon one of its intimate by-ways where birches are mirrored in the dark green waters of the swamp where one can see wild ducks; the pungent smell of wild currant, the heady scent of the balm of Gilead, and the delicate fragrance of the lady's slipper are still fresh in my mind. And walks to the beach to watch the graceful, gray gulls glide overhead while the busy little sandpipers flit across sand flats along the water's edge. These are but a few of the aesthetic facets of Waldron in the springtime. Above all, I remember the profound stillness and fresh air.

How quickly the scene can change from placid, shimmering waters and sunset radiance when Mother Nature puts on one of her splendid displays of elemental fury. The sky and sea seem to meet in a study of black, white and grays; the lowering clouds go scudding by, while the waves, heaving into deep arcs, break on the beach. Like mighty giants they lift huge logs as though they were mere sticks, disbursing them in wanton abandon foaming and flashing while the spindrift sweeps in sheets that sometimes reach the mountain top.

It really isn't a mountain, just a precipitous headland of shale, sandstone, and conglomerate. Point Disney rises like a sentinel from the deep water of Cowlitz Bay. There are several ways to reach this promontory. There was an old road leading up to "Whispering Pete's" place; he was dubbed this name because of his stentorian voice. You could see the remains of his log cabin and an eight foot cedar rail fence. The deer, in his time, abounded on the island until some of its inhabitants became greedy. They would use their dogs to round them up for the kill; a remaining few were known to swim away to another island. There had been an apple orchard and one tree continued to grow over the years; its pale green tips could be seen trying to reach the sun in competition with the tall second growth timbers.

Another way led through a second orchard and when the plums were ripe you could help yourself; this was before the advent of the crow and pigeon explosion. The plums were an extra premium and a little refreshment for the trek ahead, up the abrupt rise of narrow sheep trails, over several ledges and outcroppings to the lush undergrowth of salal, blackberry, and wild rose bushes, across the moss-carpeted terrain to a grove of stately Garry oaks.

This is the highest point of the island, about 580 feet; the rest of the way is a gentle slope out to the point. You may stop to see the eagles' nest as you approach their domain, and if it happens to be spring there will be wild flowers in profusion. It is sheer enchantment to gaze out upon that panoramic view of sea and sky and the surrounding islands, the distant Olympics, and the misty mounds of Canada.

No matter where you go on this rather special island each little area has its own aura of charm, whether it be a simple log cabin in the woods or a chalet overlooking the bay, a long stretch of sandy beach covered with silvery drift, or the magnificent majesty of Mount Baker and the Sisters in the afterglow of a summer day.

Chapter One
Meet The Mate
1933-1934

My Jim was a man of few words. In a journal he kept
containing items of interest during his seafaring years, he
recorded the cold, unadorned fact of our beginnings
together with just two words: "Got married." Short and to
the point, like his voyage letters to his company, Jim was
not one to waste words. He was not exactly a scotchman,
although he said one time that he was half scotch and half
soda; just a little joke among friends.

He wasn't completely seasoned, not yet an old salt, but
he had hopes of someday becoming a captain of any vessel,
of any tonnage, and of all oceans. He had already served as
junior officer on the S.S. *Pan American*, a passenger ship
running to Buenos Aires, and had sailed on several other
ships, increasing his status to Chief Mate. But it was in
1933, during the depression, that Jim and I, in a state of
just-married bliss, had a problem. He was "on the beach," a
seaman's expression for waiting for a ship; that is, without
a job.

In the meantime, Jim's brother, Phillips Lovering,
wrote to us from New York asking us if we would like to
make a honeymoon trip to Washington State and look
over some eighty acres of land that he had just bought on
an island in the San Juans. His friends, June and Farrar
Burn, had written him that the land was for sale, so he
purchased it site unseen.

This sounded like an adventure. We eagerly laid out
maps and charts on the floor of our San Francisco apartment and while on hands and knees we started to search
for a little-known dot on the map which was Waldron. We
found a small seagirt island in the northwestern-most part

of the San Juan archipelago, bordering on Vancouver Island, Canada. To us it seemed like the last frontier and as remote as any far-away place to which Jim's travels around the world had ever taken him.

I had never met Phil; he was the eldest of the Lovering clan and a gentleman of the old school. He was a smart, young, civil engineer who had also known the frustration of being unemployed. Phil was very family minded, although he never married; his reasoning was that if things got too tough, we could make out somehow, living on those eighty Waldron acres that cost him most of three months' pay.

So while Jim waited for his ship to come in, we became involved in the family plan. We discussed the possible means of a livelihood on Waldron in case we liked what we saw and decided to stay. Raising chickens was one option since Jim's uncle Albert ran a large hatchery in California and offered to start us out with day-old chicks come springtime. After much deliberation we decided to go take a look see.

It was a long and tiresome bus ride and it was not until midnight that we arrived in Bellingham, Washington. The town was in total darkness due to an electricians' strike. To make things worse and adding to our dismay, we discovered that our luggage had not come on the same bus with us. We felt a little awkward having to ask a man on the street corner where we could find the Leopold Hotel, and more so when we asked for a room; we explained our dilemma to the night clerk who was understanding and helpful in giving us a room. He also provided details of how to locate the mosquito fleet that made their runs to the islands.

Navigation was Jim's forte so we had no trouble finding the path to Quackenbush dock at Whatcom Creek, which led us through Old Town across the railroad tracks and boardwalks. I felt a little clumsy in my high heels and we must have been an odd looking couple dressed in our city clothes.

We found the wharf bustling with activity in the early morning hours. We watched the M.V. *Osage* and her smaller sister ship, the M.V. *Chickawana*, as they loaded on their assortment of freight and mail sacks and, lastly, a few passengers. It was a beautiful fresh morning in late August. After making our acquaintance with skipper Homer Irwin and deck hand Art Flaherty, we climbed aboard the *Chickawana*, whose motor was warming up with a slow chug-a-chug that increased in momentum as we pulled out into the stream . . . "I think I can make it, I think I can make it," it seemed to say, then faster "IthinkIcanmakeit IthinkIcanmakeit," and so forth. It was a five hour ride and for the sum of just fifty cents we were to receive our introduction to the lifeline of the less populated and far out islands of the San Juans.

Bellingham Bay is famous for its turbulent waters and running tides, especially in the prevailing southeasterly wind, but this day nature was on her best behavior; not a cloud in the sky and the air was warm. Jim went up to the wheelhouse to talk shop with the skipper and to take a few soundings while I sat out on the deck drinking it all in and feeling the pull of its magic as this little mail packet wended its way through open stretches of water, through Peavine Pass and its shoals and narrow channels to the Orcas dock where they pulled alongside for a little ship's business. Then off again through narrow Pole Pass with its submerged rocks which this seasoned crew seemed to flit across with much expertise. Next we skirted the Orcas shore, crossed over President Channel, and arrived at Waldron about noon.

The coming of the mailboat was probably one of the most exciting events of the day for these people who were so dependent upon it for so many things. They had no ferry service, electricity, or telephone, so the skipper and his mate were like members of the family, bringing and taking messages, calling a doctor, or alerting the Coast Guard in times of emergency.

Pilings were being replaced in the dock when we arrived so we were lowered into a rowboat for our trip to shore. We were met on the beach by the Burns with welcoming smiles. Farrar had a long beard and June's hair flowed down to her waist. The rest of the natives looked on, giving us the once over as they unloaded their freight and feed.

With a toot of the whistle and a wave of the hand, the *Chick* took off across Cowlitz Bay for Prevost Harbor on Stuart Island, her next stop. From there, their course took them down San Juan Channel to Friday Harbor, the county seat of the islands. Here they hove to for the night, making a return trip the following day.

In one of her columns for a Bellingham publication, June once wrote that there were forty odd people living on Waldron, and some took exception to it. True, we found a few eccentrics but most of the people became our long-lasting friends and neighbors. I learned years later that on that first day they had doubted we would last more than six months on the island.

We met the very gallant and gentlemanly farmer, Gavin McNaught, who drove us across the island in his horse-drawn buggy to Fishery Point where June and Farrar lived with their two sons, North and South. We spent a couple of idyllic weeks there, sleeping in a tent on the sand flats, eating mush made from whole grain wheat that June ground from her stash in hundred-pound sacks and served with whole milk fresh from the cow. Her specialty was "hoe cake" made of corn meal, baked over coals of an open fire, and smothered with fresh-churned butter. We tasted our first dandelions, nettle greens, and miners' lettuce. Farrar taught Jim to bring in the salmon. It was so easy in those days just to row out into the flooding tides with a hand line, hook, and sinker, or maybe a Pearl Wobbler.

During this time we met William and Elizabeth Chevalier and their little brood, Marge, Betty, and Billy, who were near neighbors to the Burns. Elizabeth was the daughter of one of the first pioneers to come to the island and had a wealth of knowledge of its history and early times. Her sister, Louise, also native born, was married to Stanley Gale and they, with their two small children, were to be our neighbors. We met John and Margaret Severson and their children. Margaret, who also came from one of the earliest homesteading families, was wise and soft spoken. Ethan and John Allen and many more would have a hand in weaving the fabric of our lives.

We landed on this island with about two dollars in our pockets and September was already upon us, so we realized that we had to face the facts of life and look to the real purpose of our visit. The property Phil bought and asked us to look over was on a southwest slope and had a huge barn made of immense timbers and poles sided with handhewn cedar boards. There were two small chicken coops, a ten-by-twelve foot log cabin and a small woodshed. The one room shanty that we were to occupy, made of two-by-fours and shiplap, was built by Joe Fernette. After his death it was used as a bunkhouse by loggers. Despite the huge task of renovating this humble dwelling, our decision was to stay.

The place was dark and dingy, the roof leaked, and several window panes were broken. The furnishings consisted of one table, a broken chair, and an old mattress on the floor. The cookstove was dirty and greasy; the firebox and oven were full of holes. June had tried to make it more cheerful by painting the door a bright blue and by putting some colorful nasturtiums in a broken teapot on the table. My upbringing, in a family of ten kids with rather meager means, gave me the fortitude to tackle what lay ahead of us. My father used to say when we were faced with some difficult task, "Just put your ears back and look savage."

Jim's immediate task, however, was a little more difficult. His quarters aboard the training ship, the *U.S.S. Annapolis*, I am sure, were above reproach; and there's no doubt that the several ships he sailed were shipshape. Although his excellent education was of the sea, his need now was firewood. For this, he was unprepared. At first he gathered any dry twigs or rotting windfall which, as it turned out, wouldn't hold a fire even in the best of stoves. After he acquired a few tools and supplies, Jim "came to" about the different trees—that red fir was the best for stovewood because of its pitch; alder was good too, but it needed to be split while green and left to dry. It was not as plentiful as fir. The white fir was only good for the pulp mills.

Jim was carrying the wood in four-foot lengths on his back about a quarter of a mile to the house until he found an old wheel with the shaft broken out. With a few ends of boards, peeled poles for handles, and twenty cents worth of nuts and bolts from Roy Crum's emporium, he made a dandy wheelbarrow that made his job easier. With a possible northeaster in the offing, our need got beyond the wheelbarrow stage. It was then that Harvey Allen, sensing our need, came to the rescue. He helped Jim clear out a path in the dense undergrowth to some larger trees and with his seven-foot crosscut saw they bucked up three cords of wood in jig time. Another bachelor and friend in need, Charlie Fahlstrom, hauled it down with his team and wagon.

In the meantime, I was learning a thing or two about saws; you needed a different type for each job. There is a crosscut saw, a rip, a seven-point, and a five-foot, hack saw, buzz saw, a keyhole, and a jig saw. What was once a puzzle to me soon became routine. I also learned to make bread. It may be the staff of life but without water you are sunk. Fortunately there was a good well close to the house and, as a friend of mine said, "You had running water if you trotted with it."

Another family we met was that of Mary Wood of Boston, her three sons, Ralph, Lester, and Cecil, and her daughter, Gertrude. Mary's husband, Fred, died before we came. He was the nephew of old Ned Wood, one of the most colorful and widely travelled of the early goldrushers and homesteaders, the story of whose exploits usually ended in mystery. The most likely one is the oft told tale of Ned's pot of gold that he dug into whenever the need arose. It is periodically revived by the younger gold-digging generation who let their imaginations soar as they dug deep, but to no avail. Ned died in 1906. The ivy, which now grows in such profusion on their old house and buildings, is claimed to be from clippings which Mary brought with her.

Ralph Wood had been a muleskinner in the army and had a way with a team of horses, although I'm sure they didn't always understand his language. He also had a gift for water-witching. It was not to be very long before we availed ourselves of both these capabilities when the well ran dry and a man with a team was needed to grade and pull out logs from the woods for our new building. This log structure was to serve as a store, post office, and a place for island social affairs, dancing, Easter breakfasts, Thanksgiving dinners, and New Year celebrations. But this is putting the cart before the horse.

The island folks had been right in their prediction. On the 15th of December we awoke to five inches of snow. We were as exhilarated as any of the kids and went out in it making and throwing snowballs at each other. The snow didn't last long for it was followed by the southwest wind. I thought it would pick up our shanty and carry it away. It was too rough for the *Chickawana* to come and everyone was shaking his head and murmuring, "Worst in forty years."

It finally cleared before Christmas so the school went ahead with its program. The enrollment that year was just seven, namely: Marge and Betty Chevalier, North and South Burn, Pete Gale, Carol Severson, and Alice Johnson. Louise Myers was the teacher, fresh out of Bellingham Normal School. Her salary was forty dollars a month and people added to this with such things as eggs, vegetables, fish, and an occasional poultry handout.

Just before Christmas the wind swung around to the northeast and it was bitterly cold, freezing everything in its path. On Christmas morning we were awakened by a knock on the door. It was our postmaster, Roy Crum, bringing us a special delivery letter, rather a rarity for Waldron but nothing urgent as he had feared. It was just a Christmas message of good tidings from home. We thought it was a generous and neighborly act on his part to come out in such weather.

June and Farrar Burn invited us to have Christmas dinner with them and they also asked the bachelor brothers, Jim and Gavin McNaught, who donated a goose for the occasion.

The Burns had come to the island in 1919 from Maryland and homesteaded on Sentinel Island, another little dot on the map that had lots of rocks, trees, and solitude, but no fresh water. I wouldn't exactly call them settlers as they didn't stay in one place very long at a time. They were the roamingest people I ever met. They had some guardian angels on Spieden Island who watched over them until their boys were born, and later they bought their place at Fishery Point on Waldron where they made a home and the boys went to school. It was not very long before they moved on again. No matter how far and wide this lively young couple would roam, they would keep returning to the islands of their first love for inspiration and refreshment.

June was well initiated into the art of cooking over an open fire, but a goose? . . . no supermarket, pre-basted butterballs then! If you wanted a goose you couldn't be choosy about it, you simply went to the barnyard, chose your quarry, and, if you could ignore those beady bright eyes, you gently laid its head on the sacrificial block and with one decisive swing of a sharp ax—I wouldn't want to spoil anyone's dinner; this, of course, was all done behind the scenes. The downy white feathers had to be plucked dry, the pin feathers removed; then after a soap and water bath, and a good scrubbing, your goose was ready to be cooked.

We bundled up in all the clothing we could muster and walked the three and a half miles to the Burn's cabin. It was crackling warm and bright inside and decorated with sweet-smelling cedar boughs and fir, snowberries, and rose hips. June had a thing about anything that was not natural; no tinsel or ornaments. Their young sons, North and South (South preferred to be called Bobby) had put up a tree and there were gifts for everyone.

Being replete with plum pudding and all the other delights, we were now treated to some of Farrar's songs and guitar playing. He was a real troubadour and entertainer and June had a sweet voice to accompany him. One song I shall never forget; it was about their cow, Janis, which was to be our first animal:

> Wait 'til the cow goes dry
> and we don't have to milk her for a spell;
> We'll turn her in the clover
> 'til the honeymoon is over;
> Wait 'til the cow goes dry . . . etc.

We had planned to go caroling around the island but it was just too cold and had started to snow again, so we made tracks back to our own heatless habitat.

Step by step we adjusted ourselves to the simple life, working from dawn 'til dark, cutting and peeling poles for an added bedroom and a lean-to for a kitchen. We repaired fences and made a new picket enclosure around the house and orchard to keep out the cow and the sheep.

I'll never forget our first cow, Janis. We had some of Charlie Fahlstrom's heifers using the pasture and when we turned her in with them there was a terrible to-do. They tore up and down the field, chasing one another until I was fit to be tied. I asked Jim if he couldn't stop them. Janis was with calf and I was afraid she would lose it. Little did I know about such things, that it was natural for Janis to establish her territory. She was the victor.

At times we had our misgivings as to whether we could do justice to Phil, our benefactor, who was always patient and encouraging. But there were always compensations — the joy of our first bedstead that Jim made from some lovely knotty cedar, and what fun it was when our wayward luggage and a trunk from home arrived. There were such goings on as I happily (and a little crazily, thought my mate) waved my cologne atomizer around the room and gleefully puffed up billows of bath powder, sending its sweet smelling feminine softness into all the smokey corners. When we finally acquired a stove that didn't smoke up the place and a secondhand Aladdin lamp, it was pure bliss.

There were a lot of "first times" for us. We purchased ninety pounds of beef, fore and aft quarter, from Charlie Fahlstrom for which we paid $5.10! It seems incredible now. When I saw it lying in front of me in all its nakedness I gave a little shudder, girded up my loins, and went in for a tackle with the butcher knife. With the help of my sidekick, Louise Myers, the school teacher, we pitched right in, cutting into chunks the sirloin, T-bone, filet mignon, and the less savory pieces with unmerciful impartiality, packing it all into jars, adding a little salt, and sealing them with the now old-fashioned glass tops and jar rings. We then popped them into the old wash boiler and cooked them for four hours. It was quite a job, but such satisfaction to see seven quarts of beef and the same amount of soup on the larder shelf and some fresh meat left over. What a change from canned corn beef and Spam! We tried our hands with clams. I was a little squeamish at first and would cut away everything that looked distasteful to me, such as the neck and stomach. As my grandkids would say, "Yuk!" But I learned.

There was one thing for which I needed no introduction—the meadow mushrooms. When I was a girl in England, my mother would take the family for a holiday to a little thatched cottage in Wales. It was sheep country and we would go out in the early morning to gather mushrooms. I remember that our path always took us through a cow pasture and one time there was a herd of black cattle that we had to pass. But not me; I was petrified! Anything that big on four legs was a bull to me and I would walk five miles around another way rather than go through that field. When we came to Waldron and had a cow of our own, I thought differently.

I loved to sit on the rocks at Mail Bay in sight of Mt. Baker and fish for rock cod. According to Al Charles of the Lummi Tribal Council, the Indian name for Mail Bay is Schishuney, meaning "Fishing place with a pole." For a long time I never tackled a salmon; I left that to the menfolk. One year there was an extra big run of hook-nose silvers in the Bay, and after I canned eighty quarts and salted down a barrelful, I said to Jim, "Don't you dare put another fish in my sink." He then tried to persuade me to come with him, saying, "You might enjoy it!" I thought that I didn't have the patience (Jim always had enough for both of us) so, although I had not been convinced, I went along, bundled up to the eyebrows against the chill of the evening. I was rigged up with a fancy pole and was introduced to the workings of a reel and how to hold it, and there I stood on the stern of the boat thinking how boring it all was.

Then it came, that first tug on my line. I hollered for help but none came. Jim was busy bringing in a fish of his own, so off came the scarf, sweater, and gloves as I warmed up to the thrill of playing and reeling in my first salmon. From then on I was hooked.

Chapter Two
Roots And Shoots

My father, Frank Edward Wood, liked to tell people that he came from a little island off the coast of France. He was referring, of course, to the British Isles. He was an Englishman born in Bhagalphur, India, on the river Ganges in sight of Mt. Everest, the highest mountain in the world. He was brought home to England as a child to be raised and educated in the county of Kent.

Father chose at an early age to follow the sea. He served his apprenticeship on sailing ships that took him far and wide across the oceans of the world. He was just twenty-one when he left England as second mate on the *Dovenby*, a brand new ship sailing to Australia. From there the ship went to San Francisco where she was laid up for three months waiting for a cargo.

Seafaring was rugged in those days and most of the sailors jumped ship without their pay, leaving a skeleton crew. The idleness, for one so young and energetic as my father, became monotonous so he asked to be paid off. He went ashore in San Francisco and found work on a ranch in San Rafael and joined the "Sons of St. George" for recreation. There he met a young lady named Frances Lucinda Marthis, who was out west visiting a cousin.

I know little of my mother's origins except that she came from hardy mid-western stock – railroaders and cattlemen. She and the young Englishman went dancing and dined at the famous Cliff House in San Francisco and it wasn't long before he asked for her hand. They were married and went back to Lincoln, Nebraska, where her folks lived and where their first son, Frank, was born.

After the death of my dad's father, he was called back to England to receive his inheritance, which should have been a considerable sum, since my grandfather was Charles Bell Wood, an indigo dye merchant, and from a notable family. The young couple, fairly floating in rose-colored dreams, set off from Nebraska for Liverpool with their young son and with high hopes of collecting their fortune but, alack and alas, as so often is the case, their pot-of-gold was a mere will-o-the-wisp, whittled down by the barristers-at-law. So it was back to the Eternal Sea for my father.

The ways of the English were a little strange for my mother at first. She was very lonely, but the babies kept coming which gave her little time to brood. I had a very happy childhood. My mother could play the piano and sing like a lark. Sundays were set aside for church and Sunday school and it amazes me still how she could send us off in our starched white frocks and pinafores. Mother did most of the sewing of our clothes. When my father did get home from the sea, he would take us for excursions in the country, often walking as far as eighteen miles. If we got tired he would let us ride home on the "puffa train" as we kids called it, laden with wild primroses, cowslips, and anemones. We would hear the skylarks far over the sand hills among the sweet briar roses or delight in the rolling surf at the seaside and gather cockles and mussels at low tide. Dad used to offer a half-crown to the first of us to find an agate. One time my brother, Charles, while hunting agates, found a half crown. It was the equivalent of a quarter, but to a little lad it was a fortune.

I remember the tidy little rows of brick houses separated by walls which encompassed a place for a garden. At the head of the street where we lived, there was a park that had formidable looking iron gates which the parkkeeper locked each night at nine after a bell had been duly rung. It had a man-made lake where graceful white swans slowly paraded by and where we sailed our paper boats. Around the lake there were gardens, with drifts of golden daffodils and crocus in season, with a background of flowering trees. There were cricket grounds, bowling greens, and a field where we kids would play rounders. It was a game similar to American baseball but was played with a tennis ball and a flat bat.

The system of schooling was different too. The boys went to a separate grammar school and the girls attended an elementary school. The nine grades were referred to as standards and were compulsory. Any further education was up to the family or individual according to their means. I received a scholarship to a higher elementary school and, judged by American standards, I had the equivalent of two years of high school by the age of fourteen.

After World War I, my mother had a longing to see America, the land of her birth and remaining family. Over the years she had told us of this great and wonderful land so the thought brought great excitement. It was impossible for the whole family to go at once so we were divided up. My two older sisters, Mabel and Madge, baby Marian, and my two younger brothers, Theo and Reginald, and I were chosen to come with mother, leaving two sisters, Geva and Ethel, and my brother, Charles, to follow with my father. My eldest brother, Frank, was keeping up the family tradition and following the sea.

We were quite a "Woodpile." On April 1, 1920, we went aboard the White Star Liner, S.S. *Baltic*, and said goodbye to the jolly old British Isles.

On the voyage over we encountered some huge swells that rocked the boat from stem to stern. It was something like a roller coaster giving that same feeling of exhilaration, that breath-taking descent, then the abrupt rise that you could feel in the pit of your stomach. My sister Madge and I, with some other passengers, were up in the prow of the vessel fascinated by the glistening sun on the deep-green rolling sea, when suddenly the ship lurched and we were engulfed in a tremendous wave. I thought this was "Goodbye, world" as I found myself disappearing into the ocean, but, as the ship righted itself, I was being washed down the deck. I was fortunate in only getting a good scare and a thorough soaking while my sister was knocked unconscious, and several other passengers were injured. Thereupon that section was roped off and for the rest of the voyage it was off limits.

Perhaps this little episode, and the fact that I was susceptible to mal-de-mer, could have been the reason for my being a poor sailor; but this didn't stop me from being attracted to my blue-eyed, curly haired sailor Jim, who was to become my mate on the ship of life.

Jim came from a rather imposing background; on his mother's side was James Albert Hawke, for whom he was named. This distinguished gentleman was a medical officer in the Union Army during the Battle of Gettysburg and later with the U.S. Navy, retiring as a Rear Admiral. Going back to the 1600's, his ancestor John Howland was one of the signers of the Mayflower Pact.

His father, Phillips Adams Lovering, was a medical officer in the U.S. Navy during the Spanish American War. His great, great grandfather served as a page boy for the Boston Tea Party at the age of twelve. Jim and Phil, too, were brought up under the strict regimentation of Navy life. Coming home from school they had to salute their father, saying, "Reporting on board, Sir." It was ingrained into them to have a deep respect for their flag, which was raised and lowered at their home every day.

Jim was quite an enterprising young man and unbeknown to his family, earned a job as second pantryman on the S.S. Manchuria, an ocean liner headed for New York. When the ship arrived in port, it was met by his uncle from Philadelphia, who took the young maritime aspirant under his wing, saying if he wanted to make a career of going to sea he should do it the right way.

Jim already had the necessary qualifications for entering the U.S. Naval Academy in Annapolis, and in due time passed the required examination but for one physical technicality. As a young lad, a splinter of rock had pierced his eye leaving a small scratch on the eyeball which prevented his entering that worthy establishment. As an alternative, Jim entered the Pennsylvania Nautical School for four years of merchant marine training.

Fate had some peculiar ways. If it hadn't been for that little rock, I would never have met my mate. But I did, and here we were, living on an island, with all sorts of adventures and lessons still ahead of us. We learned, for instance, to watch the clouds and be aware of the winds, and the tides, for living on an island you are dependent upon the whims of the weather. You begin to feel it in your bones, so to speak.

Chapter Three
Early Homesteading
1860's – 1932

In most every new venture in this life there is an element of pioneering, but not all pioneers come in sunbonnets and covered wagons, crossing rivers and mountains and encountering hostile Indians. There were others who came later. After reading the histories of those people and hearing their stories in my own time, I feel very humble in the face of these courageous men and women who came from far and near to make a better life in the San Juans, and on Waldron in particular.

There were many reasons why they came; it is part of man's nature to look for greener pastures and here they could fill their souls and feast their eyes upon Waldron's pristine beauty. Their need was quite basic and there were gifts from the sea to satisfy their hunger. The waters teemed with fat herring and abounded with salmon, cod and halibut; shellfish was plentiful under the shingle, and there was virgin timber and wild game on the land which could be had for the taking and proving of a claim.

The first settlers on Waldron, John E. Brown and Sinclair McDonald, chose the west side of the island, a long stretch of beach extending from some sand and clay bluffs to Sandy Point. Brown was a Pennsylvanian who, before discovering the island in the 1860's, had a mail contract and a farm in Alaska where he had done well. He was a bachelor and he built a sturdy house of fitted logs with rafters fastened with wooden pegs. He included rifle ports as defense against marauding British Columbian Indians. The sandstone chimney and fireplace still stood when we came some 75 years later. He had put in a large orchard and the trees had grown immense. I recall finding a quince tree that still bore fruit from which I made jelly.

McDonald, on the other hand, who recorded a patent the same year as Brown, was a bachelor from Gainesville, Georgia. He had hoped to make a stake in the California gold rush but failed, and was also unsuccessful in the Caribou country, so he too settled on Waldron as a neighbor to Brown.

In 1870, Eduard Graignic and Louis LaPorte, two French sailors who were looking for a better way of life than the rigors of sailing the briny deep and the shipboard fare it offered, jumped ship in Victoria, B.C. They crossed over into Washington Territory, landing at La Conner where they met two Indian maidens, Lena and Louisa of the Swinomish tribe, who became their wives. The couples spent several years looking for just the right spot to make their homes, and they knew they had found it the moment they set eyes on the glistening sands of Waldron's North Bay between Sandy and Fishery Points. The herring setting into the shore there seemed inexhaustible, and they soon had a thriving herring smokery.

Lena Thomas was only fifteen when she married Ed. She could neither read nor write, but she raised a large family, learned to cook and sew, knit sweaters, and had a fine vegetable and flower garden. In later years she gradually went blind but was still able to get around with a cane and was a better fisherwoman than her daughter who, she said, would do the rowing while her mother would land her own catch without the aid of a net. With hard work and perseverance the family prospered and Mr. Graignic was able to make a trip to Paris from whence he hailed.

As their families grew so did the farm, as they had planted apple and cherry trees and green crops. Lizzie was one of the Graignic family of thirteen, only six of which grew to adulthood. She would tell us how she remembered her father making the little boxes in which to pack the smoked herring and the little sticks he would whittle to string them up on. They sold them for 20 cents a box. They caught dog fish, rendering them down for their oil which was used to grease the skid roads for logging. Frank, their eldest boy, became a deaf mute after a childhood illness, but it was uncanny how his other senses sharpened. He developed a shrewd knowledge of the tides and eddies around the island, and he could bring in a salmon 'most any time of the year. Another brother, Pete, was also quick to learn the ways of the unfathomable deep, and at the age of seven he was entrusted to sail the family sloop, *City of Paris*, to Canada and Bellingham where they would market the herring, fish oil, halibut, and apples.

The wiliest of the boys was Prosper, who also had the salt of the sea in his veins and the cunning of a fox. In his young manhood his path took him through some stormy seas and into many fast running tides. It was in an era when honest money was hard to come by, an era of smuggling and rumrunning. You might not be able to condone breaking the law, but you had to admire Prosper's daring and courage. The ardor and bravado of youth usually settles down and so it was with Prosper; after he had paid a small debt to society, he married and settled in Sooke, B.C., still following the sea as an engineer in the fishing industry. His sister, Marie, also married and moved to Sooke.

We were to come to know the Graignic family quite intimately. When Louise married Stanley Gale, they moved onto the old Trueworthy place and were our nearest neighbors. Frank stayed on the island most of his life while Lizzie cared for her mother. The seven other children of Eduard's, who either never saw the light of day or died of an accident or sickness, are laid to rest in the little pioneer cemetery at Sandy Point, their graves almost indistinguishable in the ever-growing underbrush and crumbling fences.

Lizzie's story would not be complete without telling of the Ed Chevalier beginnings, which is so beautifully presented in *Pig War Islands* by Dave Richardson. It was just as easy to go by canoe or sloop to visit other islands, Spieden and Stuart, as it was to mush through the brush of their own island, especially when there was an attractive young man in the picture. It was by this means the Ed Chevalier's son, Bill, and Lizzie met and in the course of time were married. They lived in Seattle for awhile then returned to Waldron just a year before Jim and I arrived. Their youngest offspring, "Little Billy," was to play an important part in the fulfillment of our lives.

What started out to be the makings of a happy family for the LaPortes came to an abrupt end when two of their youngest children wandered out into an open pool and were drowned. About the same time, Louisa was left a widow. The memory and associations of the location filled her with such an overwhelming sadness she felt she must have a change of scenery. With her other two children, Cornelius and John, she took up a claim around Fishery Point on what is now know as Severson's Bay.

As the moth is drawn to the flame and the herring to the light of beach fires, and as the Frenchmen had been attracted by the herring, so people attracted more people. They seemed to come from all parts of the globe. The three Thomas brothers, who installed the first fish traps at Fishery Point, also attracted John Kertula, a native of Finland who knew a thing or two about hunger and the rigors of climate in his early childhood. To him, Waldron must have seemed a veritable Garden of Eden. In due time he met the widowed Louisa, and with his special aptitude for finding the best locations for fish traps and she having the rich bottomland on which to farm, together their story had a happy ending. They had one child, Margaret, who became Mrs. John Severson. Margaret seems ageless for at this writing she is still living on Waldron, hale and hearty, in her eighties.

When John Brown died in 1882, being a bachelor and having left no will, his homestead was divided among his heirs, Ed and Mary Gilshannon and Mary's brother, Bill Trueworthy. Ed and Mary had eight children who soon outgrew the log cabin that Brown built. Chapters could be written on the lives of these people and how they battled against wind and tide and swirling currents to stock their staple supplies. At one time Ed Gilshannon was given up for lost in San Juan Channel on one of his trips back from Friday Harbor. His sloop was recovered by Frank Graignic; evidently it had capsized with his sacks of flour and sugar. He was later picked up by the steamer *Islander* on Brush Island in the Gulf of Georgia.

Little is known about George and Jenny Dingman except that George became Waldron's first postmaster, using their little shanty in the center of the island for an office. The postmaster had to walk two and a half miles across the island to Mail Bay, appropriately named, row across treacherous President Channel about three nautical miles to Eastsound, pick up the mail and retrace his steps with the mail sacks on his back. This was done twice a week.

Sinclair McDonald was the next postmaster and he served for seven years. He used his dwelling place to operate the mail business and also perhaps some shady dealings of his own. His pious solicitations on behalf of supposed "missionaries" brought in contributions of clothing which it was rumored he sold to the Indians and Chinese. A man has to live.

As more and more seekers came to settle, the island map was beginning to look like a patchwork quilt, becoming more colorful as each claim was worked into place. It spread into a growing community and then came the old snake in the grass, taxes, raising its ugly head. As the need for schooling loomed, the bachelors beefed about paying out for those who had not yet proved their claims. There was a great deal of resentment and some of them lost their claims over it, and others went into debt and were unable to pay the twelve percent interest on delinquent taxes. Ed Graignic personally hired a teacher in 1894-95 for three months in the winter. School was held in a small claim shack on the Lyle place, which eventually went for taxes.

The eighty acres that Jim and I first came to live on had once belonged to Joe Fernette. He and his brother, Charles, were French Canadians who came to the island in about 1890. Charles and his wife, Anna, settled on the adjoining eighty on the southwest slope near the present dockside overlooking Cowlitz Bay. Joe was a bachelor, but Charles had a family of seven girls. His wife, Anna, became postmaster after McDonald and served in that capacity for 35 years, the longest term in the history of Waldron to this day.

Charles passed away before proving up his land and Anna neglected to do so, which posed quite a problem when Jim and Phil sought to purchase the land. Charles had built quite a large frame house and I remember the big pear tree with its spreading branches on the south side of the house, the lilac bushes, iris, and rambling roses that at one time had been the garden, and a large orchard of apple and cherry trees, prunes, and plums that stretched across several acres.

When a company interested in quarrying sandstone had leased some of this land, several more buildings were erected, most of which had long since fallen into disrepair. One had been used as a dining hall for the quarry crew and later as a clam factory. Its roof was caved in and I thought it an eyesore. I wanted Jim to tear it down but he said it was full of treasures that might come in handy sometime. This was out of my realm but it was a time when any old piece of scrap iron, chain, or a nail had its value. He finally tore it down, and with the help of the wind the roof collapsed; still he saved every usable board and hammered away at the bent nails until they were reasonable straight for re-use.

The school problem was compounded by the arrival of three families with many children and future potentials. They were German-born immigrants full of vigor. Fred Krumdiack, who first came and saw, sent for his wife,

Louisa, and family, and took out a claim to the north, bordering on the Kertula place. With the help of some Japanese laborers they built a rugged, hewn cedar log house that is the most substantial pioneer home left on the island. Fred was elected to be Waldron's first constable.

Soon the relatives began to arrive and Ferdinand Baatz and his wife, Marie, settled a claim across from the present school grounds. Fred's half brother, Ernest Rayhorst, and his wife, Mary, homesteaded on the east shore just south of Point Hammond.

A few years later came a young man of a different caliber, a graduate engineer from a mid-western state college who added his patch to the ever-growing spread. Ed Allen (no connection to the Ethan and John Allens who came later) showed his community spirit by donating land for a school and a plot for a cemetery close by. He left sometime later to serve as the San Juan County engineer. In the meantime, a small building was used for the school for 23 years, but it was far from adequate for the ever-growing population.

Chapter Four
The Chicken Comes First
1933-1934

Waldron was never destined to become a boom settlement with business prosperity. No matter what kind of enterprise was started, it seemed to peter out. The early homesteaders had reaped the crop of its natural resources; the wild life, forest products, and sandstone. By the sweat of their brows they claimed all the free land. What was needed now was that medium of exchange, money, with which to pay for the land and taxes and simple needs. The only jobs available were those of postmaster or teaching in the one-room schoolhouse, and these were pretty meager at best. There was farming and fishing in season and a little day labor here and there.

People have tried to live in a dream world, eking out a living from the land, eating roots and shoots and a little fish, but even the most rugged individualists and romantics sooner or later have to face reality. So often the San Juans are referred to as "the isles with the unhurried atmosphere," and when Jim and I first set eyes on Waldron we may have harbored such thoughts in comparison to the mainland. But we learned that there were not enough hours in a day to do all that was expected of us.

First we attended to the leaky roof over our own heads and made a place for the cow. We cleaned out one of the coops for a few chickens which Farrar gave to us in exchange for a setting of eggs from a super record-making rooster that we bought in Bellingham for one whole dollar. So the die was cast; we were in the chicken business. We planted an orchard and pondered our pasture needs, did some slashing and seeded it with wheat and vetch. We leafed through government bulletins on how to raise chickens. We cut and peeled poles for a 20 x 40 foot chicken house and feed room. Times were lean and every penny was to be accounted for to Phil, the silent partner. Jim had to give up his tailor-mades, rolling his own with Bull Durham. I was a real scrooge.

Some people called us greenhorns and we were, in this field, but we were about to show them. We took the plunge and ordered 400 day-old White Leghorn chicks. I never thought I would care for farm animals, but when a little calf was born or when I saw those little woolly lambs, my heart softened. Cows can be ornery critters, but they are only doing what comes naturally when they try to hide and protect their offspring. When Madge arrived (we named all our heifers after my sisters), Jim had to comb the whole back forty looking for her, traipsing through the woods and the dense brush, then carrying the little squirmer down in his arms while it struggled and kicked.

We weren't exactly ready for the baby chicks either. The brooder we got from Sears had been set up in the old log cabin, but we didn't know that chickens were like children who had to be cuddled and coddled and given their cod liver oil and vitamins. Our 400 little yellow balls of fluff were all wanting food and water after their long journey from California. We were up half the night adjusting the temperature and watching that they didn't crowd and smother.

Jim's uncle, Albert, had quite a system: setting the eggs at the hatchery at a given time to coincide with the date of delivery; with assembly line precision he had them hatched, packed, and on their way to the mails the same day; they arrived on the *Chickawana* three days later. By this time they were ravenous.

Like all little things on a farm, they grew and needed more space to spread their wings. They outgrew the brooder and were put on the range. The pullets were separated from the cockerels, which kept flying over the fence. We had to clip their wings many times until they were doomed for the market or the frying pan.

When the pullets reached the laying stage, they were put into the new henhouse; the nests were darkened for privacy, the gypsum laid out on their doorstep for cleanliness. We felt pretty proud of our accomplishment, only having lost three birds out of the original 400. We ate so many cockerels we thought we would sprout wings.

We were dependent on our neighbors for the spring plowing, not having any equipment of our own, but I spaded up a spot and with a copy of *Farm Garden in the North* (a government bulletin) in one hand and a trowel in the other, I put in some early stuff. I found seed catalogs the most fascinating things. That first year when most seeds were five cents a packet I sent for five dollars worth; just about everything in the book. I had seed for the next five years, almost.

One fine spring morning I had just set a batch of bread to rise when Ruth Allen came knocking on my door asking if I would do a little "sewing job." There were no doctors on the island and somehow I was elected. Jack's hired man had almost severed his thumb while shearing sheep and Ruth had brought along an old rusty surgeon's needle that Jim shined up and sharpened on his emery wheel while I steeled myself for the ordeal. I boiled the instrument of torture with some white silk thread and went to work. The man's endurance was remarkable for he was without the benefit of pain killer or even a shot of whiskey which the oldtimers would have used. As I tried to penetrate his tough skin pulling the severed edges together and tie knots, he never once winced. I had doubts about myself, but after five or six stitches I was joking with him, asking if he preferred hemstitching or herringbone. I tied nine stitches in all and his thumb healed miraculously, with no after-effects. As for the bread—that was one batch that was never kneaded.

Jack's brother, Ethan Allen, took us under his wing and taught us many things: that lambs had to have their tails docked, and the fine art of shearing—even I tried my hand at it, the lanolin makes your hands so soft! You can become quite an expert if you keep your thumb out of the way.

"Old" Ethan, as we called him, was well known as the *Sage of the San Juans*. He claimed to be a direct descendant of the great American patriot of the same name. He and his wife, Sadie, had taught school in Indiana but Ethan wanted to make history, not teach it; not for any fame it might bring to him for he was the simplest of men with a philosophy and belief in the Almighty by which he lived.

Mr. Kimple of Orcas Island remembered when he first met the Allens as they were coming from Eastsound pushing a wheelbarrow which they had borrowed to carry their trunk of worldly goods. They had walked the two and a half miles over the same route as the first postmaster had taken. Mr. Kimple rowed them across the two miles of channel over to Waldron where they homesteaded a claim just south of the Mail Bay property. Several years later they acquired some of the most coveted land on the island from the Doucette bachelors, who happened to be in a disgruntled mood over school taxes. Gold seekers who had been disappointed in other areas migrated to Waldron during this time and took up homesteads. These properties changed hands several times with each new owner seeking the impossible dream of riches, not knowing that they stood on the very brink of it. Their land, especially the lots on the waterfront, would be very valuable. Consequently Ethan Allen hit the jackpot, buying the whole 440 acres for $500!

It took a lot of potatoes to make the payments on the land so Ethan accepted the school teaching job. All that was required for the three months in the year were the three R's, but for this broad-shouldered young man with a cause, it was not enough. Working towards his goal of bringing the 27 island schools into the county system, he visited these schools making the rounds by watercraft in all kinds of weather. He, too, learned about the tides and swirling currents, treacherous channels, and waterways.

Sometimes after figuring the tide, he would have to leave during the night, sleeping in his boat until the school he was going to visit opened. Sadie would help him with the teaching at home and Ethan was made the County Superintendent.

You might say he was a self-educated man with a tremendous grasp of history and science, although he never went to college. He had a few essential books and a dictionary which he said was all that he could afford. He was full of wit and how often have I heard him say, "Just lief not know so much, as know so much that ain't so."

We did not know Ethan's wife. She died just before Jim and I entered the picture. They had two sons, Ethan, Jr., the teacher counterpart, and Harvey, who became a fisherman and boat engineer.

Shortly after Ethan was settled, his brother, John (or Jack as he was more familiarly known), came to visit him. He looked over the land of tall timbers and unexploited earth. He set his heart and mind on some acres overlooking Cowlitz Bay and worked for the next six years for the Pacific American Fisheries on Eliza Island, saving his money until he had the purchase price of $1,250 which Sinclair McDonald had insisted must be paid in gold coin. Jack procured the necessary pieces from the San Juan County Bank and the land was his.

In 1905 he married Ruth Doty, or "Sugar Plum," Jack's pet name for her. She was the daughter of a then well-known fur trapper and trader on Sinclair Island. Jack brought her to Waldron as a bride of 19, carrying her across the threshold of the old log cabin that McDonald had built. No time for honeymooning, no frills or fancies, just plain hard work from the beginning.

Life was hard and Jack met the challenge with day and night laboring, raising corn for his pigs and oats and hay 'til his barn was bulging. Jack also operated a small store where the inhabitants of the island could buy staples in the evening when the day's work was done. He was out for every penny he could make and wasn't above doing a little moonlight bartering across the border in Canada, taking over eggs and produce and bringing back sheep's wool.

When their family began to grow, Jack added on to his original acres and purchased the Gilshannon place where he built a simple frame house overlooking the bay. Today it is devoid of any tree, shrubbery, or flower, stark and windswept and with not a whisper of all the love, laughter, and tears of children who grew up there and went away.

One day Jim bought an old skiff and pair of oars for $5.50. He thought it to be in pretty good shape and seaworthy; all it needed was a couple of planks in the bottom which he fixed in his *spare* moments. We were expecting Jim's mother and his sister Stella and wanted to take them out fishing. He also built some steps down the steep embankment that led to our own special beach where we could find agates most any time. This beach was nestled between two high ridges of sandstone and conglomerate rocks and in one hidden nook there was a cool spring of water trickling down the rocks where maidenhair fern, bright yellow musk, and Indian Paintbrush grew in the crannies. The view from here takes in the wide sweep of the Haro Strait islands, and we could watch the big ocean-going liners on their way to and from the Orient. At these times I seemed to sense a wistfulness about my mate, a vague yearning perhaps to return to his first love, the sea.

For the time being, at least, he was content with taking me for a ride in his skiff. We went for our first swim here and it was our favorite spot to dig clams. On a very sunny day after a minus tide, the sea coming in over the warm sands would be quite pleasant, and the rock ledges gave us a perfect diving board. Later, when our daughter Franny came into the picture, she would pull on my skirt and say, "Come on, Mommie, let's go down to the sandy beach, it's just like dishwater." It was little interludes like this that made life worth living, giving us inner strength for the myriad tasks and problems that were ahead of us.

You learn patience on a farm, for after you have sewn your seed you must wait for nature to perform its miracle and have faith that things will grow. Our garden flourished and was a thing of beauty, producing its tender vittles in their season. I had been saving the first picking of peas for when the family came, so early that morning I went to reap my reward—Oh! Woe was I, the cow and sheep had been there before me! Not a pea left in the whole patch. Just one of life's little vicissitudes, although I doubt if those were the exact words I used at the time.

Finding and developing a new source of water seemed to be our next most pressing need. Jim and Andy, a man we hired to help, located an old skid road that Ben Briggs used when he logged off the place. It became one of my favorite haunts, walking under the tall second-growth firs and cedars, amongst the dainty lady fern and infinitesimal wild flowers which grew out of the moss-covered remains of the fallen giants of the forest, and where the sword and bracken fern grew as high as your head. The wild black-berry vines cascaded over the fallen branches and their fruit hung in mouth-watering profusion in their season.

At the end of this wooded copse and up the rise a way, the men experimented with several damp spots until they found a likely flow of water. It was necessary to wall up the spring with rock to hold back the earth which at times was like quicksand and which kept caving in. The men grubbed through 1400 feet of entangled roots and rocks to make a trench for the pipe that was to reach the house, barn, and chickenyard. A great deal of engineering know-how had been employed and all types and costs of pipe and pipe fittings taken into consideration. Fortunately the path of the pipeline was on such a gradual slope that the water came down by gravity with no need for a storage tank, engine, or pump.

Up to now we had no means of transportation except what we could get for hire from our neighbors and at their convenience. There was feed, groceries, lumber, and kerosene to haul up from the dock and soon cases of eggs to ship off the island.

During the ranch's history of old second-hand trucks and farm machinery, we were harassed and confronted with breakdowns and worn-out parts, but Jim was really ingenious when it came to conjuring up something out of nothing, or from his treasure-trove of junk.

First came the wheelbarrow, then the skiff, and now a Ford coupe which was for sale on the island. His mind was running wild as to how he could fix it up to best meet our needs. It was some sort of a racing car with *ruxtel* gears but Jim saw its possibilities, wrote to the boss with his ideas, and with his sanction bought the vehicle for $35. Jim cut out the rear end of the body and built on a truck bed. Then, rigging up a buzz saw with mandrel and pulleys, we had a contraption with which to do the hauling, cut poles, and saw the winter's wood.

My mother had never been convinced that I was happily having the time of my life here. She wasn't quite sure it was the place for me. The idea of having no facilities, carrying buckets of water from a well, and scrubbing clothes on an old-fashioned washboard dismayed her, but she underestimated me as being a chip off the old block. She decided to pay us a visit and check things out, coming with my father and brother, Charles, and the so-often-used phrase of today really applied: they fell in love with the place and could hardly wait to find out if there was any land for sale.

It was I who now felt concern for them; they were getting on in years, and in case medical help was needed our only recourse would be to row a couple of miles across the channel in an open boat to telephone the doctor in Friday Harbor, or, if the occasion called for it, to send for the Coast Guard.

I wasn't one to cross my bridges before I reached them, and it was a couple of years before they found 38 acres which they bought for back taxes, and a year or so after that before they came to settle. They did as most pioneers did; built a little log cabin in the woods, made a garden, and raised a few chickens.

The fall of the year could enchant most anyone with its autumn coloring, its breathtaking sunsets, and Indian summer, its ripening fruit and that indescribable aura in the air. This particular year had been a time of joy and exploration, of learning and discovery. It had been a long hot summer and our little fruit trees and oats had suffered. If we had lamented the lack of rain then, it was now soon to descend upon us. In November the unpredictable southeaster brought torrents of rain and the westerlies. Wow! We learned early that Waldron had no safe harbor for small boats and Jim got soaked and clonked on the head trying to rescue his precious skiff. The wind shifted the shed on the dock about ten feet. The ton and a half of baled hay it was housing was all that kept it from being whisked clear off the pier.

At three a.m. we were awakened by a loud thump and we were sure that the roof had fallen in. A large strip of tar paper was ripped from the roof, landing just outside our window. The rain simply poured into the house and then suddenly the wind shifted to the northeast and temperatures dropped, putting everything into a deep freeze. This was a prelude to winter. Digging for the pipeline came to a standstill while all our energies were directed to keeping the hens happy and the cow contented.

The second onslaught came in February and it was a dilly. We set up the brooder in the bedroom to help keep things from freezing; we ran out of kerosene, our water buckets four feet from the stove had two inches of ice on them. We were concerned about the eggs, but those pullets went right on producing them as though nothing was happening, with an average of 80 to 200 eggs a day. Jim had to take out hot water every two hours to melt their drinking water; we were running out of cases in which to pack eggs and our feed was just about exhausted.

The brave little crew on the *Chickawana* had started out from Bellingham, but they weren't able to make very far and didn't get to Waldron for ten days. Whenever there had been a lull in the wind, they would make a dash for a cove in the lee. At least we were living high on the hog, so to speak, having butchered the pig. We made out on head cheese and sausage.

It had all come so suddenly and there were so many things to try to protect. The canned goods in the cooler and the potatoes and apples in the root cellar were all frozen. Still, the show must go on; we had a lot of irons in the fire and it kept us hopping to keep one step ahead of each new project and chore.

Chapter Five
The Quarry Boom
Early 1900's

At the turn of the century, Waldron was quite a growing community with several large families and an assortment of bachelors and single loggers. The herring run that sustained them earlier had begun to diminish, but the need for logs for the lime kilns on San Juan Island was a great help to the economy and the cordwood industry was in full swing. Like the herring, the forest supply seemed endless. For instance, Fred Krumdiack cut four logs one time, two of which were 16 feet long and two were 18 feet that contained 10,000 feet of lumber for which he was paid $85.

Just about that time Ethan Allen unearthed more of the island riches when he discovered a vein of coal on his land, but the island was to be spared the development of that deposit when gold was discovered in Alaska.

This northern discovery was to have its effect on the San Juans and Seattle. The need for better streets to accommodate the on-rush in Seattle sent quarry men in search of sandstone. In those horse-and-buggy days, better paving material was in demand for Seattle's steep hillside roads. James E. Riley from South Dakota had opened a quarry on Stuart Island and took out sandstone which was used to pave Jefferson Street. Then it was discovered that the entire south end of Point Disney was composed of a very fine quality of sandstone, so, with a contract in his pocket for Yesler Way, he moved his operations to Waldron. He built a bridge-like structure from the quarry clear around the face of the cliff where they loaded the scows. Workmen wheeled the blocks out onto this bridge. The paving stones, roughly one foot on a side, were shaped by hand with a shaper having a blade at one end. Each stone had to be cut an exact width. Blockmakers worked by the piece, sitting on stools on the beach. Riley paid them seven cents a block employing between 30 and 40 men who earned extra money by loading the scows when the tides were favorable.

Things were going fairly well until Savage and Scofield, a large and powerful company from Seattle, got wind of the operation and the magnitude of the sandstone deposit. They also had unearthed the fact that Riley didn't own the shorelands in front of his quarry, so taking out a 45 year lease on the land, they simply took over one day when they knew only the cook was on the place.

The new company brought in its machinery and donkey engines and went to work blasting the Point into a rubble. They used five old windjammers with their masts cut short to barge the stone, towing them to Seattle by sea-going tugs. The last of the quarrying was done in 1909 and the island began to recover from this dynamic enterprise. The land that was left belonged to the Joseph Sweeny estate.

What they had done to Point Disney must have been a sorry-looking sight. It had once been one of the San Juan's most outstanding and awe-inspiring works of nature. It could never be rebuilt by man but nature has a way of healing its wounds. The rubble rots away in time; grass and little trees spring up. The birds were jubilant with their new rookery and nesting place and there were new holes for the rock fish. It had not been all bad; true, it had brought in rats, but the rats killed the mice (small consolation) and people could gather the remains of sandstone blocks for building for years to come.

The quarry brought regular boat service from Anacortes twice a week and the county built a dock at the end of the road so that the daily mail service to the islands was possible. The people became less isolated with this link to the mainland.

Busy, busy Jack Allen supplied whole carcasses of beef pork, and mutton to the quarry workers, carrying everything on his back a mile hence. Besides farming and keeping his store, he had little time left for the amenities of life, but he always had a kind word for the ladies, declaring, no matter how old, that they were looking younger every day. Years later when he was no longer in business he was known to have said he couldn't understand why people weren't able to make money running a store. In his day he boasted of having a credit rating with Dun and Bradstreet.

The men who came to participate in the strenuous and hazardous quarry labor were predominantly of Scandinavian origin. They worked hard and played hard and were fun-loving; they helped the islanders build a large community house where they could dance. There were between 100 and 150 men and some of them formed a "Swede band" that became quite popular in the county; people from other islands came to join in the fun. Sadly enough, this building was demolished when the roof caved in during one of the worst storms the islands have known.

Most of the men left after the quarry closed, but a few remained to settle on Waldron and become part of the community. John Severson married Margaret Kertula, and Ed Borg married Josephine Fernette. George Lindsey, the bull cook, was an unknown quantity; a bachelor and a loner taken to some strange ideas with not much love for his neighbors whom he called Huns and Bolsheviks. He had a place by the school grounds and years later he died of starvation.

Herman Olson, on the other hand, one of the powder men, was a very pleasant person. He bought 40 acres next to the Dahlbecks and built a small cabin and barn. He was quite a horticulturist; besides putting in an orchard he experimented with many special trees and shrubs, even a persimmon tree that bore fruit. It was the need of money again that made it necessary for Herman to go off the island and work in another quarry, a move that was his undoing. He went in to inspect a charge of dynamite that had not ignited, when the blast went off in his face, almost blinding him. He sold his place to a German family by the name of Selke and bought a little parcel of land behind the school cottage where he carried on his plantings and lived a fairly useful life until his cabin burned down. He had been groping around in the dark and knocked over his kerosene lamp. It was surmised that he couldn't find the one opening in his shack. His remains were found in the ashes.

Fred Norby tried his hand at farming on what we now refer to as the Adrian place. He married a mail-order bride, Bessie Gustafson. Ethan Allen, who was by now the justice of the peace, officiated.

Fred had a bachelor friend, Charles Fahlstrom, who came from the same island in Sweden. Like so many before him, Fred was so taken with the life on Waldron that he wrote to his hometown paper urging more people to buy and settle here. Charlie, who was then in Seattle contemplating a move to the Sacramento Valley, read the ad and passed along the word to the Dahlbecks, who also came from Sweden and who were then in New York raising their family. Subsequently they came and each bought 40 acres.

While the effects of the quarry extravaganza were receding into the past, life went on as usual. The men went back to their cordwood cutting and the logging, and the women continued to have children and chores.

Next thing on the agenda was the old issue of a larger school. The bachelors were still against it, but the mamas and papas won out. In comparison to the original building this was to be an edifice, complete with a bell in the belfry. The high-pitched roof was the conventional red while the outside was painted white. On two sides of the building there were tall windows all the way across, making the most of the sunshine and daylight. A tall flagpole was erected and firmly embedded in cement. The huge maple tree that graces the school yard was planted on Arbor Day in 1894 by Ethan Allen and the children. It was a little Canadian Maple seedling that they tended with loving care and it grew and grew, and the children climbed and swung in its branches. Time means nothing to these monsters of the tree world.

Chapter Six
Growing Pains
1935-1939

Jim was always thinking big. He figured that if we could do so well with 400 baby chicks, why not try a thousand. He wasn't a gambler in the usual sense of the word, but he sure was an optimist.

Early in 1935 when the old Charles Fernette place adjoining us went up for sale, Jim recognized it as a golden opportunity to secure this land at a reasonable price, so he lost no time in engaging the services of a good lawyer. The legal aspects were many and involved as Mr. Fernette had never filed a homesteading claim and died without leaving a will. A court hearing was necessary to establish the claim and to get the release of the family heirs. After a sale price was agreed upon by Mrs. Fernette and Jim, the final deed and clear title to the 80 acres was soon in the hands of the Lovering brothers.

The next thing on the agenda was to fix a place for the increase of chicks. Jim converted the barn using half its space, put in windows on the sunny side and set up an extra brooder and a cot for himself. You might say he went to bed with the chickens for the first four or five days, keeping the night watch and setting the alarm every two hours to check on conditions. Meanwhile, back on the farm, there was the cow to milk, chickens to feed, eggs to gather, clean and pack. It was time for spring plowing and seeding. The sheep had to be rounded up from the mountain for shearing and another chickenhouse had to be built. Mr. Meenach, the county agent, was so impressed with our chicken achievement that he suggested I keep some poultry management records.

It was plain to see that we needed help and it was

presently forthcoming. My brother, Charles, who visited us the year before, was looking for a change of scenery and thought Waldron would be an ideal place to raise his family and, perhaps in the near future, to open a nice store. He had a good deal of experience in hardware and store management, was a good mechanic, and an enthusiastic worker. He wrote to Jim asking him what he and Phil thought of the idea.

We, of course, were sensitive to the presence of Roy Crum, who came to the island during the quarry boom. He ran the Waldron Mercantile store with all his eccentricities, his moldy merchandise, and his reluctance to sell the last of a kind in case another customer would ask for it. In spite of these things, he was liked in the community, although at times he swore that people were robbing him. If it is right, a thing has a way of working out, so for the time being we shelved the idea of a store and welcomed Charlie and his wife, Georgia, and two small sons, Bobby and Jimmy.

They found plenty to do, fixing up the small building which had been the office and commissary of the quarry days. It left a lot to be desired but at least they had running water, and what a location—with the beach just a stone's throw away. Charlie pitched right in making himself useful in many ways.

Jim was having his troubles getting the hay cut. There had been a long dry spell and then it had rained for a week. The Ford blew a gasket and he had to borrow Ethan Allen's horse. Then the wagon shaft broke from sheer old age, so Jim had to cut the last of the hay with a scythe.

The young chickens were getting in his hair; they were all over the place, scratching in the garden, roosting in the highest beams and in the tallest trees. He simply couldn't control them and it made it very difficult to catch them when it came time to put them in the laying house. This had to be done under cover of darkness and took many nights.

But time and tide went relentlessly on and the forces of fate held their sway. The chickens thrived and a new chickenhouse was in the process of being built. Things looked rosy. We were expecting our first child, but a dark cloud came to overshadow our happiness; what was to have been our shining hour turned out to be our first mortal sorrow. The little fellow came too early and his nameless little body was buried by the woodshed.

Time is the great healer and my mother, who was with us at the time, was a great comfort. Jim's sister, too, was very sympathetic yet was such cheerful company.

There was good fishing that summer and we went out in the skiff and I was kept busy canning salmon, beans, and corn. Stella had sent me a pressure cooker—I was afraid of it at first, but I got used to it. It was such a time saver and took the guesswork out of canning.

The harvest had been good except for the cherries; the crows were getting thick, no doubt having a banquet from the chicken feeders on the range. Waldron in those days had few predators except for the crows, an owl or two, and a few chicken hawks. The little cottontails, *Lepus Sylvaticus*, came later. Roy Crum swore he had seen a cougar one day when he was on the mountain; he had felt its hot breath on his neck! When he went to shoot it, so goes the story, he slipped and his gun went off. He claimed he carried the bullets in his back the rest of his days. The cougar may have been a figment of his imagination, but the bullet could be seen by x-ray in his last days.

The island had a herd law; if you didn't want other people's stock to come trespassing, then you had to fence in your place. Since that was easier said than done, we let our sheep roam at will on the mountain with the rest. Once a year a group of neighbors would get together and have a round-up for marketing, docking, and shearing.

Except for a minor accident when Jim cut his foot with an ax, this winter was kinder to us than it had been the previous year. It was either milder or we were more prepared for it. We had passed the tenderfoot test.

The year 1936 was another one to remember. First the men completed the new 16 x 24 foot brooder house with space for an eggroom and a screened-in sunporch. It was such an improvement over the makeshift arrangements of the previous years; it was heated by a wood burning hot-water system which proved its efficiency and economy. Still, Jim had to do his stint on the couch, getting up to stoke the boiler every few hours. Uncle Albert sent him 1,062 babies this time and that was quite a nursery.

It was a cold and wet spring and April brought heavy rains, but it also brought a little recreation for Jim. He had made a canvas sail for Harvey Allen's boat so they took a day off to try it out, making a trip to Friday Harbor. Sail-making was one of the crafts Jim had learned at the academy along with the ancient art of square-knotting. Sailors did this long before *macrame* became a fad; essen-tially they were the same, but aboard ship it was used for more practical purposes. Sailing down to Friday Harbor doesn't sound like much of an outing, but in a time of such simple diversions it could be the epitome of pleasure.

May brought the flowers and June the roses and the cow brought forth her first calf, which we named Mabel. Then it was my turn. I had been brooding a little chick of my own who was in such a hurry to try her wings it really caused a commotion. It was one of those days, everything happening at once. The county agent had come with the veterinarian and his assistant to test the cows for Bangs disease. Mr. Wheeler, the carpenter from Orcas Island, had arrived to begin work on the new log building, and there were extra helpers to feed all around. It had been a crucial time for me; Dr. Kite had warned me against undue activity and had been checking my condition once a month, coming to the island from Friday Harbor in the Coast Guard cutter that was stationed there in those days.

It was a great blessing and comfort to have my sister, Madge, with me through this difficult time, taking all the household chores upon her shoulders, but, on this day, it was just too much to expect of her—I felt that I must pitch in and help.

Once again Jim had to man the oars and cross the channel to alert the doctor, who came the following morning, advising Jim to get me to Friday Harbor without delay. Being a Saturday, the *Chickawana* was heading in the opposite direction, so Jim went after Bill Chevalier who had an open boat with an inboard motor. There was yet another delay, the wind was blowing a stiff westerly so we sat on a log on the beach until it calmed down a bit. It called to mind what Ethan Allen had told us—how he and his wife, Sadie, were in a similar situation when their first son was just about to be born and he really meant *just*; how they had to sit on the beach waiting for the tide to change. He had a three-hour workout at the oars ahead of him, their destination being Anacortes. He had remarked, "You can do a lot of praying in that length of time, but you can't do anything about the tide."

Lizzie Chevalier had come with us and it was strange that I should feel such a calm. The storm within and without had passed and we were on our way.

Dr. Kite was new in Friday Harbor and it was to be his first maternity case. I had called him a devil-may-care southerner but he was to prove himself somewhat of a saint. I stayed at Jean Hook's home (she was the registered nurse and midwife at that time) and after long hours of labor and chagrin, I was delivered of a three-and-a-half pound baby! When I first saw her, I said, "Ugh! A girl." I guess I had given my deliverers a bad time, doing some loud protesting during the process, but then it had been a dry birth and one may say some strange things under such stress. She was so tiny; had to be fed from an eye dropper, and during the first nights she started to turn blue. From then on she was my treasure, my little cherub, and all those special things only a mother could dream up when that magical moment comes to hold her precious little bundle for the first time.

Forty-two years later I visit occasionally with Jean and Laurel Hook and reminisce about old-times. The house where the birthing took place still stands on the corner of Guard and Tucker streets, painted a bright red with white trim and the same rambler roses still grow in profusion on the fence. On the opposite corner, where the Mormons now have their meeting place, is the house where "Little Billy" Chevalier came into the world. With the face of Friday Harbor so rapidly changing now these two places hold a special significance for me, the lowly beginnings of a little girl and boy destined for each other.

Dr. Kite had not wanted to become a doctor. He had done so to please a maiden aunt of his; he had just wanted to be a farmer and raise a garden. Jean remembers that when the time came for him to assist in the delivery—he had disappeared! She frantically called his home and office, and then looking out of the back window she saw him up in a cherry tree sampling her cherries.

When Jim came back to visit me and the Wee One, I asked him, "Well, darling, how have things been going at home?" and he replied, "Oh, just fine, honey, just fine." "Oh, yes," he continued, "Don (he was the hired man) let the Ford over a 50 foot bank and demolished it, and a bunch of us went to Deer Harbor for the dance and Ralph Wood stood up in the boat and fell overboard." It had been too rough to come home so they had put up at Kimple's beach for the night. I was thinking of the expense of that little escapade; not that I begrudged Jim a little fun, but the Ford! What would we do now? When the tears began to well up in my eyes, he said, "Why, honey, whatever is the matter?" That was my Jim—sort of happy-go-lucky. I was the worry-wart, the Pisces, and he the Scorpio. I could always depend on him to give me assurance that things were never as bad as they seemed.

When it came time for us to leave Jean's tender care, Jim hired Jack Douglas to take us to Waldron; Frances

Estelle, as we had named her, had gained half a pound so I wrapped her up and put her in a shoe box for the journey home.

For several days I was nervous with my small responsibility. The living room floor was still wet with fresh paint. We hadn't been expected so soon so folks at home, in their zeal to have everything nice for the little stranger, had almost painted us out of the house. We managed to squeeze into our one small bedroom and lean-to kitchen and I gave baby her first bath in the dishpan by candlelight; there had been no coal oil for the Aladdin.

With each day I gained strength and confidence for my new role and routine. Meanwhile, the farm was teeming with new life and activity and progress was being made on the log store building. Jim found a second-hand Dodge sedan to replace the ill-fated Ford and he converted it into a truck. Then Jim had another bee in his bonnet. This time he was thinking of a portable sawmill. He reasoned that with all the chickenhouse lumber we were going to need, it might be less expensive to cut our own; he could make it all sound so convincing. For the moment there were more immediate chores to keep the men busy but the idea was given some thought.

After building an egg room and some range shelters for the pullets, Jim, Charles, and Mr. Wheeler concentrated their energies on finishing the new log building. They had the roof on by Christmas. It had been tedious and exacting work; cutting, peeling, and fitting each log into place, but it was a work of skill, brawn, and beauty. Jim hired a stonemason to put in a large fireplace which was constructed of field stones and granite. It was all in keeping with the rustic surroundings, facing into the south and west with a wide veranda on two sides overlooking the Bay. Framed by a large madrona tree, the picture was complete.

Charles was quite elated to see his dream come true and it lifted everyone's spirits as we viewed it with the pride of accomplishment. It had been a rather dreary winter, with piercingly cold northeasters and snow. At times we felt so cut off from everything; when the *Chicka-wana* couldn't make it and the wind howled around the old house, which, with every gust, we feared would be carried away.

The thought of fire breaking out in our isolated state with the lack of equipment and shortage of water, could strike fear into the stoutest heart. One morning the roof on Charlie and Georgia's house caught fire. Charles was in the woods and Jim was on his way to the dock when some-one yelled that the cottage was on fire. When we arrived on the scene, he found Georgia up the steep roof trying to beat the fire out with a pair of Charlie's pants which she had been washing. When someone passed her a bucket of the washwater she was using, Georgia exclaimed, "Oh, I can't use that; it's too dirty!" A little humor can go a long way to ease the tension, whether she was in earnest or not. It could have been disastrous—the shingles being old and tinder dry. As it was, it burned quite a hole, which meant another immediate chore for the already overloaded men-folk.

Georgia had another emergency and when the doctor was brought over, he found it necessary to perform minor surgery for a hemorrhage. He asked me if I could admin-ister the chloroform. I gulped, saying that I would try. It is wonderful what you can do when you have to, but my knees were shaking and, confidentially, I was scared. Albeit, there were happier times in store for us.

By the time June rolled around, things had slackened off a bit. The store was open for business and the pullets were out on the range. Jim said that he could spare me for a little while. I had a golden opportunity to hitch a car ride to Berkeley, so I took off with the Wee One. She was at such at cute age, just taking her first steps and I wanted to show her off to my family and friends. I had sisters all over the Bay Area and I was able to see my sea-going brother,

Frank, whose ship, the *President Coolidge*, just happened to be in port. After spending eleven days in Berkeley I went up to the ranch in Calistoga where Jim's uncle and aunt had the hatchery from whence came our baby chicks. This was indeed a happy day for Jim's mother, who was seeing her first and only grandchild for the first time.

We had Franny christened in the little church in St. Helena where Jim and Phil grew up and attended school. Jim's mother and her sister, Mabel, left for Waldron before my visit was up. I returned by train.

Jim had fixed up the old log cabin for extra company, raising the door and building a small peaked roof above it; he put in two bunk beds and his mother thought it great fun climbing a ladder to reach the upper berth. The inside walls were covered with smooth boards. On the outside, a mass of colorful sweet peas was climbing up its walls.

The two ladies had adapted themselves very well in my absence but they found the housekeeping rather involved, having to cook on a woodstove, skimming milk and making butter, scalding milk pans, and making cottage cheese. We now had two cows, a heifer and a steer, and we were shipping cream to Friday Harbor.

The completion of the "Waldronia Store," the name we had decided upon, called for a celebration and we had a supper party for about 20 people on the wide veranda while Jim's folks were still visiting. It was a farewell to the young folks who were leaving the island with their families to attend high school and for North Burn who had been spending the summer "batching" with a couple of buddies. It was one of those balmy mid-summer evenings, not a ripple on the waters as we watched the sun go down in all its glory. There was dancing to follow and as the evening wore on a big moon rose over Point Disney, casting mystical shadows and displaying its silvery light across the land and sea.

I remember the old phonograph records we danced to and I had tried to explain to North the fundamentals of dancing as we awkwardly tried the basic one-two-three steps of the waltz. He returned years later, tall, suave and self-confident. He reminded me that it was I who taught him his first dance steps.

Everyone declared that they had a wonderful time and clamored for another dance the following week. From then on it was more than a store building—it was a meeting place, a fun place, with recreation from the monotony of chores; a comfortable place to sit in the shade in the summer; and in the winter there was warmth by a big log fire while waiting for the mailboat to arrive. Surely people couldn't object to this; still, even way back then there were a few who were afraid it might bring modern ideas to the island.

In September there came the most distressing news that Jim's mother had passed away suddenly of heart failure. It seemed incredible—it was only a few weeks ago since she was here with us alive and well, but "The Lord giveth and the Lord taketh away." Jim left for Calistoga where the family had gathered for services. Mrs. Lovering was buried in St. Helena, the town that had been their home after their father retired from the Navy.

Jim's younger brother, Joe, came back to the island with him for a short stay. He was a medical doctor and had received a fellowship to further his career at the Mayo Brother's clinic in Rochester, Minnesota where he became a practicing surgeon. The pig we were fattening held a strange fascination for Joe. He would lean over the fence and admire her saying she was a beautiful creature. As he watched her, he tried to determine whether she snuffed her food through her snout or slurped it through her mouth. It may have had some clinical significance for him, but I couldn't share his enthusiasm except in terms of smoked hams and bacon.

In October my father and mother decided to take the plunge, coming to live on their 38 acres. All hands turned to helping them build a small log cabin and dig a well. My mother wasn't very strong but she was a good sport and adjusted to the new life. She had raised a family of ten children and that was accomplishment enough, and she was to be a great comfort and help to me. My father was in his glory, saying, "I'm a hard case, sleep in the top bunk, carry a razor to sea, and spit to windward." He was full of these sayings, whether they made sense or not, and he had a treasury of sea stories. His hobbies were gardening and geology and in his time he had made oil paintings of the many sailing ships on which he had served. It was in the autumn of his years that he found a haven, his little flat land with the sea all around.

In January of the new year Jim's brother, Phil, made his first visit to the island, all agog to see what we had accomplished. The brothers had very little time together but they made every minute count, practically going over the whole 160 acres and talking of the future of the farm and its immediate needs.

Phil agreed that more capital was needed. Farming by hand was a tough job, we needed a tractor and a plow, a disc and harrow. Jim popped the question of a sawmill and Phil was quite enthusiastic; he was always one to take advantage of the materials on hand and there seemed to be plenty of second-growth timber on the place.

We decided to sell the sheep, all but a remnant which remained on the mountain, and to clear some of the fields of rocks and stumps for better pasture. It really was scary when the men started to blast, especially when a charge failed to ignite. There were a few anxious moments when Ralph Wood went to check the fuse. One blast sent a huge stump flying through the air, hitting the roof of our house, knocking off the chimney pipe!

Ever since Phil's visit, I could tell that Jim was feeling restless and dissatisfied with the contribution he was making to the family cause. He wasn't afraid of hard work but his training had to do with the sea rather than the stony, stumpy land. Yet with things still in a state of depression we were fortunate to be where we were. Nevertheless, Jim made a trip to San Francisco to check things out and got some encouragement from the Coos Bay Lumber Company, on whose ships he had sailed in the early '30's. He returned in better spirits and started to pursue the mill idea.

He located and cleared a site and made a bed for the mill engine. Sometimes I thought Jim was a descendant of Job, his patience knew no end. In frustration, I sometimes felt that the island must have a special spirit that objected to the invasion of machinery and that delighted in harassing anyone working with it. When everything was set up, the saw in place, and the men ready to cut some lumber, the quarry-vintage Ford engine that Jim had hoped would do the job went berserk. A connecting rod sheared off and the piston dropped down and came through the side of the crank-case. Jim went to Bellingham to look for another engine; he found a 100 horsepower, eight-cylinder Stutz, equipped with power take-off pulley, all set up on a frame ready to go. Ironically, it had to be taken apart so it could be shipped on the *Chickawana*. This cost us the large sum of $54.30 plus freight.

Jim had received the promise of help from the Martins, who had a small mill on Orcas Island. The very day he went over to get some pointers, their mill burned down; they were as good as their word though, and Mr. Martin's son, Avery, proved to be the key that turned the trick. With his expert help it was not too far in the future before we had our sawmill operating and producing not only timber and shakes for our own use, but planks for the county dock.

In the meantime, things were happening at "Crum's Castle," as people called it. Roy had part of an acre across from us. It was mostly rock, and on the water's edge he had erected an establishment that resembled an old ghost town building with a false facade. In March, Roy got the urge to travel back to Iowa, closing up his store and leaving Frank Graignic, the deaf and dumb islander, in charge of the post office, saying that he would be back in a few days. After a month had passed without hearing from him we became concerned, but he eventually sent us a picture postcard of a voluptuous bathing beauty, assuring us that he was having a wonderful time and would be back shortly. Roy's "shortly" stretched out over another month. Frank's livelihood was fishing and when it came time for him to leave he asked my brother to take over for him. Frank had written to the powers-that-be of the situation but they had not responded. An inspector finally came and installed Charles as postal officer-in-charge until things could be straightened out. Roy was in big trouble with the Post Office Department when he finally did return, but it didn't faze him. He had a mania for building things; he was free now to erect his contraptions. Among other things, he had built a pig pen, chicken coop, and cow stanchion, but nary a pig, cow, or bossy was in sight.

Charles received his appointment as postmaster on May 26, 1938, and the office was then set up in our new building where it has operated continuously for over 40 years, although there have been many changes in post-masters.

This seemed to be a record year; record heat, record drought, and record company. To add variety to our well-spiced life there was a fire on the island. Ethan Allen had some slashing that had been smouldering for a couple of months and in July it blazed up again. Jim thought he smelled smoke and went over at 11 p.m. one night and found Ethan fighting the fire all alone. They worked together until 3:00 a.m., then he came home for a couple of hours' rest and returned at 5:00 a.m., working straight through until the next day. By that time some of the men from the "College Camp" who were visiting Ethan's son, and his small troop of Boy Scouts, were helping to build trails and back-firing all around the blaze until it seemed to be under control.

The next day Jim, the baby, and I went over to see

how things were going. When we were ready to return, we discovered that the fire had jumped the trail and was burning the cedar rail fence and had started out into the meadow. Attempts were made to beat it out but it broke out in several other places. After fighting for an hour, we came home to do chores and Jim got our neighbor boy, Pete Gale, to go back with him. They stayed until the fire was out.

There were some islanders who just blamed and criticized Ethan, but not one of them came to give a helping hand. I never could understand why. It could have been a disaster for the whole island. Ethan was such a kindly man, a good and generous neighbor. When I told him we were expecting some of Jim's relatives, he said he was going to butcher a lamb and with a twinkle in his eye he added, "I'll give you part of the neck." Imagine our surprise when he presented us with a whole lamb.

In anticipation of Jim's receiving his call to sea, we advertised for a couple to live on the place and do farm work and carpentry and to help me in the house. It was a lucky turn of events; like the proverbial new broom, the Housers responded, swept the place clean and were hard workers. They had one small boy of school age who helped the dwindling enrollment situation. Things were pretty well in hand when Jim received his long awaited call and he left in September with confidence to join the S.S. *Lumberman*, a steam schooner sailing between Coos Bay, Oregon, and San Francisco and San Pedro, California.

Although the job was seasonal and of short duration, at least it was a foot in the door. When the ship tied up for the winter, Jim took the opportunity to go to the Marine Hospital to have some long overdue repair work done. During his recuperation he studied for his Master's License. The Cherub and I hopped a train going southward to be with him.

My father and mother were settled in their cozy cabin in the woods and were happy having so many of the family coming to see them during the summer. Mother was in her early sixties and suffering from angina. In January, 1939, after some persuasion, she consented to see a doctor. My youngest sister, Marian, was living in Bellingham which made it handy.

Mother had been in good spirits and had some of the old sparkle in her eye and even sang a few ditties while she was having her hair fixed just before the time of her appointment. But she never lived to see the doctor. Death came gently, and Mother, heaving a deep sigh, closed her eyes after a full day and a full life. Following the gathering of the clans and observing the last rites, Mother was buried in the quiet little resting place provided on Waldron beneath the two large flowering dogwood trees.

The tenure of our capable couple was of short duration; the husband liked life on the island so well that he wanted a farm of his own. He bargained for the old Swartwood place. Leroy had died of a heart attack while out riding his horse and his wife, Eva, and her mother had just up and left. The Housers bought the land and moved the following spring; however, Mr. Houser continued to work for us as an extra hand when needed.

Our next couple, Bob and Hilda Jones, were more permanent; they caught on to the work rapidly, leaving Jim free to make a few more trips on the S.S. *Lumberman*. The ship was then sold, and Jim returned home with his coveted Master's papers in his pocket and with a new lease on life, ready to take up the reins of perpetuating poultry production and management and all it involved.

The next time Cherub and I ventured forth to the big city we too came home with an important document, a prize winning photo of our Wee One. The following is what Dr. Kite reported to the Bellingham paper when he heard about it. "County Health Officer R.W. Kite reports that little Frances Lovering, 3-year-old daughter of Mr. and Mrs. James A. Lovering of Waldron Island, was recently awarded fourth place in the national children's photograph contest." The picture of the little miss was taken while she was visiting in Berkeley. Fully 100,000 pictures were submitted by studios all over the country. A clipping from the Berkeley newspaper read, "Despite the expression of sweet calm she wore for the camera, Frances is a capricious little sprite and enjoys robustness her parents once feared would never be hers. Dr. Kite attended the mother and child at birth and says there was a doubt for a time whether the baby would live." I don't know who was the proudest of whom but I had a feeling it was a family affair.

We had an arrangement with the Joneses that worked out pretty well, having alternate Sundays off, giving both parties some free time for their own pursuits; fishing, picnicking, or whatever. Beach picnics played and still play a major part in the social life on the island and in those days we had access to practically the whole perimeter of it.

The island was becoming an increasingly popular place for small boat enthusiasts and sports fishermen. Ethan Allen used to say to most any stranger, "You are welcome to use the beaches, they really are not mine, they belong to the Almighty. He just lets me use them while I am here." Ethan shared his friendship, his biscuits, and his water which flowed copiously down his meadow.

This was the year that Irving and Marjorie French, looking ahead to their retirement years, purchased the Sandy Point property. They would be doing some building. Several others had asked Jim about buying some lumber or sawing it on shares. Lage Wernstedt was contemplating retirement from the Forestry Service and was interested in adding to his present building and he intimated that he had friends who would be interested in renting cabins. It was only natural that the thought of building them should occur to Jim and Charles as a means to supplement the store business. With this in mind Charles wrote to Phil painting a rosy picture for the future of the store and sawmill.

In the meantime, there were powers far beyond our control that were setting the stage to plunge us all into the agony of war. Its impact was to change the whole pattern of our lives.

Chapter Seven
There's Eggs
1940-1941

Over the years we had coined a household aphorism: when anyone asked, "What shall we have for breakfast, lunch, or dinner?" we would answer, "Well, there's eggs." We were getting close to a thousand a day at that time and it was nothing for me to whip up a sixteen-egg sponge or angel-food cake. The Co-Op only accepted the best for the New York market which preferred the pale-yoked eggs, just a matter of taste. They were graded for size, cleanliness, and shell texture; we kept the checked eggs and double yolks and sold them on the island for ten cents a dozen.

The eggs were collected at least three times a day and were cleaned with a light abrasive, no washing—this would have weakened the shell and reduced the keeping quality of the egg. So, by using the dry method, they brought a better price. They were packed in cases which held 30 dozen. It kept several hands busy and anyone visiting us usually got into the act. Then there were the chicken chores; the floors and nests had to be kept as clean as possible and the droppings under the roosts to be kept cleared away. This commodity mixed with straw and sawdust from the mill made excellent fertilizer for the garden and fields. This was the job that Ralph Wood used to like best; he said he didn't have to think, just shovel.

To cut down the confusion of cockerels when we received too many males in the batch, we tried sexed chickens and Jim learned how to cull out the "boarders," non-producers, and the broodies. They were separated from the flock and put into special pens or crates to be shipped off to Bellingham.

Our flock was free from disease. The County Agent attributed this to the lack of traffic from outside. He claimed that disease was carried on people's feet. However, we did have to paint the roosts with Black Leaf 40 to control mites.

By 1940, we had built six chickenhouses, enough to accommodate 5,000 laying hens, with electric lights from a gas generator. This gave the chickens extra hours to feed, consequently increasing their lay.

It was as though Phil had seen the handwriting on the wall and being a keen observer of world affairs and trends in the economy of the country, he wrote to Charles and suggested that it might be a good idea to look to the future of his family on the mainland and check on the labor market. Charles was always one to look on the bright side of things, so he did as he was bid, and left for Los Angeles. Several weeks later he sent for Georgia and the children. After long hours of waiting in line, day after day, he secured a job in a munitions factory, a far cry from the peaceful atmosphere of the island but war is no respecter of persons—not all casualties happen on the battlefield. Charles lost one of his eyes in an accident at the plant when a piece of steel with which he was working pierced his eye. In spite of this he lived a happy, hardworking, and useful life and his family was blessed with seven fine boys.

Charles was sorely missed, but by some reshuffling of the cards we managed. Jim was made Postmaster and I kept the books and helped at the store. My father was a hardworking man and what a garden he could raise!

Confidentially I was against the cabin idea but Hilda's brother, who was here at the time, was all enthused about building them. He helped at the sawmill for awhile until one day he got his fingers caught in the blade and I guess that cooled his ardor. It gave me an opportunity to use some of my homespun first aid which was to snip off one finger that was hanging by a thread and bandage two others that were almost severed. He was soon to go back to

Iowa and that was the last we heard of him and the cabins, too.

The school situation was getting a little shaky with few prospects for enrollment. The *Teacher Wanted* ad for the next term stipulated "Preferable with children." The response came from Helen Kanaar, a widow with three children, two of which were of school age. So Franny had company when she started to school in September.

I recall one incident when the teacher taped Franny's mouth shut because she talked too much. Franny had some compelling ways, too. On her way home from school she would call on Herman Olson, the blindman, saying, "Come and walk home with me, I'll get your hat," and she would take his hand. Herman wrote to us once saying, "Franny has a special power over me, I cannot resist her." She needed someone to take her past the Johnson's field where they kept a bull that pawed the ground and snorted. It was a very scary thing for a little girl; I, too, was afraid of it.

Jim and I finally got around to thinking about building a house for ourselves; our present shack had served the purpose but the underpinnings were rotting away. Originally it had no joists or foundation, just 2 x 4's laid on the ground and the siding nailed onto it. We picked a nice spot on the hill where the old Fernette house had stood and started to make plans. First we built a one-room cabin on the brow of the hill under a large spreading madrona tree with a superb view of the water. This was only meant to house the carpenter while he worked on the larger house, but we ran into some problems. Rocks and stumps had to be removed and because of the war there was an increasing amount of red tape connected with acquiring dynamite. We settled for adding a kitchen and a bedroom onto the carpenter's cabin and that was to suffice us for the duration. Then it came, the blast that was to be the demise of our poultry and egg venture. It would be hard to forget that date, December 7, 1941, when the Japanese bombed

Pearl Harbor.

Jim's first reaction, of course, was to leave immediately and find a ship, but I persuaded him to wait a little while so he could finish the house and put things in order. It was not exactly the call he was waiting for but we cannot always be the masters of our fate. There were proclamations by the Commander-in-Chief asking all men with licenses to report for sea duty, or else. The prospect of being drafted into the army had no appeal for Jim, especially with a Ship Master's papers in his possession. So Jim made his plans and in the spring of '42 he left the island to answer his country's call.

Chapter Eight
Meet The Master
1942-1949

Jim chose to join the Army Transport Service and was assigned to skipper a small oil tanker named the *Express*, sailing for the Aleutian Islands to ports undisclosed. For months on end, bored and disgusted, the crew sat on their "floating gas station" which was shuttled from place to place in those frozen wastes.

Jim wrote me about their Christmas—"We had a little Christmas tree in the mess room and drew names and exchanged gifts. We tried hard to get into the spirit of the occasion, but homesickness prevailed even though the boys tried not to show it."

I often wondered where they found a Christmas tree out there in the frozen North. It reminded me somewhat of a time when Jim and I were watching *Saturday Night at the Movies* on television. It was a lusty story of passion and fighting for freedom in new lands in the wilds of Africa. In one tender and touching scene, one of the fighting heroes presented his lady love with a tiny bouquet of flowers, presumably violets. I said to my mate, "Now, how in the world could he get violets in Africa?" and my clever husband piped up, "Haven't you ever heard of African Violets?" Wasn't that a Zulu?

Nothing is forever and eventually Jim got orders to return to San Francisco. The homeward-bound sea lanes through the Straits of Georgia and Haro would come temptingly close to home so a plan was formulated in Jim's mind to veer off course and drop anchor at Waldron. Of course, he would be running the risk of meeting the Coast Guard who would have considered his action highly irregular and he would have been taken to task to say the least; but the more he thought of it the more desirable his idea became. He then wrote to me of his scheme, telling me to have my bag packed and be ready to come aboard.

They arrived one morning in March and tied up at the dock without incident; the crew came ashore and thoroughly enjoyed themselves, going out to the barn where the cows were being milked and drinking all the fresh milk they could hold and I fed them all the eggs they could handle and they departed with a five-gallon can of milk, fresh butter, and eggs. It was a great treat for them after their sea-store rations. We departed shortly, saying goodbye to little Franny who was to stay with the Joneses while I went with my Master on down to Richmond, California. There I was spirited ashore to catch a bus for San Francisco where we were to keep our official rendezvous.

Jim's next assignment was skipper of the M.V. *Houston*, a repair ship which he took to Adak and later to Attu in the Aleutians. After several months at Attu he was transferred to the *U.S.S. Restorer*, a cableship which was lying at Dutch Harbor at the time. While on the *Restorer* they completed the laying of the cable out to the Aleutian chain and also made a trip to the Western Pacific where they went right in after the landings on Guam and Saipan, repairing the trans-Pacific cable.

After about two years Jim returned to Seattle. The *Restorer* went into dry dock and Jim sailed again to the Aleutians carrying freight on the *Morlan*. While on this ship he was picked to go to the Pribilof Islands to take in the annual supplies and bring out the quota of seal skins. The war ended while Jim was still on this trip. He then left the Army Transport Service and went with the Olympic Steamship Company, sailing as Master to foreign ports. They were bare boat charters. Soon the bottom fell out of shipping as the economy worsened and the ships were put into the mothball fleet. Jim then came home to his own little island in the San Juans.

Chapter Nine
The Changing Tide
1949

During the seven years that Jim was at sea, the war
had precipitated many changes. Gone were all our lovely
Leghorns, their long rows of houses empty and silent. The
pastoral scene of cattle grazing had disappeared and the
sawmill sawed no more.

In spite of their well-meaning promises, our managers
and helpers had flown. The Joneses had kept the chicken
and egg business at a minimum, but there came a time
when they couldn't manage alone and lured by tales of
high wages in the factories, they too made their departure,
much to Jim's distress.

The Seversons were a very patriotic family and
straight away Albert and Elmer became involved in the
war effort as boat engineers. Albert served in the Army
Transport Service for many years. The Family had lost
their eldest son, Gilbert, in W.W.I. serving in the U.S.
Marines. Their father, John, was crippled by a stroke and
passed away in January, 1947. Their mother, Margaret,
still carried on alone on the old homestead raising
beautiful cattle and a fabulous garden. Pete Gale, son of
Stanley and Louise, had joined the Army Air Force. Hilda
Jones had been made postmaster for a short time after Jim
left and she was succeeded by Carnot Ward, a newcomer.
His time was cut short by death. He was found on the
beach one morning, lying by his boat on which he had
been working.

Adele Wernstedt then took a turn at the postal wheel.
The mail service was the only activity going on in our fine
log building. The once nicely stocked shelves were as bare
as Old Mother Hubbard's cupboard and business was at a

standstill. After the Wernstedts had retired to a strawberry farm on Guemes Island, another newcomer, Helen Taylor, became our twelfth postmaster.

Things had come alive for the school once more when Charlie Fahlstrom offered 20 acres of land as an induce-ment for a teacher with children. This time they hit the jackpot, getting Otis Chalfont with his family of nine.

There were still more school potentials to come when John and Helen Taylor arrived with their three children, Rhett, Timmy, and Sandra. This family added zest and creative ability to the island, which was reflected in their six-sided log cabin which they built and named *Aeolian House* because of the winds which so frequently blew there. According to Greek mythology, Aeolus was a friend of the gods and controller of the winds who reigned over a group of islands northeast of Sicily. This cabin was graced by a huge oak tree facing into Cowlitz Bay in the path of our prevailing southeast winds.

Another interesting couple who came, saw and settled were the Tiberghiens, Ray and Mary, who had bought a little strip of island gold on the sparkling sands of North Bay where they built a small log cabin. They added a touch of elegance, charm, and stability to the ever growing community.

I, too, had been caught up in the drifting tide of events and change. In 1944 there had been no children for the school so my father and I had moved to Bellingham where I bought a house and where Franny attended school. This proved to be a more convenient arrangement for Jim, allowing him to make the best possible use of the fleeting time he could spend at home. During this time I bought a new car and learned how to drive. This gave me a brand new experience and a new freedom to broaden my horizons. When the Captain blew the whistle I jumped into my shiny new Chev and went to meet his ship with confidence.

One thing we could not possibly have foreseen was the

changing of the mail and freight service. It had become a complicated schedule involving the *Water Baby*, owned by Clyde Welcome who had the mail contract out of Anacortes, and the *Chickawana*, which exchanged mail and freight in midstream on alternating days with the *Osage*, thus completely cutting out direct service to Bellingham and leaving us no means of shipping eggs and receiving feed and supplies from the Co-Op.

Another era in the mailboat's history came to an end in April, 1948 when the *M.V. Chickawana* was destroyed by fire. It happened on its way to Stuart Island after leaving Waldron when the engine caught fire and exploded. The operators were able to save the mail sacks by getting them into the lifeboat. The men and the mail were picked up later on Satellite Island by the Coast Guard.

After the burning of the *Chick*, Bob Stuart of Decatur brought the mail to Waldron on the *Mary Bob*. Then, if my memory serves me right, Ed Peacock was next to have the mail contract. Ed and his wife, Nancy, practically raised their two little girls aboard the *M.V. Macard*, the motor vessel that they operated.

Jim had many times painted glowing pictures of the island to his fellow officers and some had expressed a desire to make a visit sometime. He had a young mate, Donald Prohaska, who was really impressed, so when shipping went into a slump after the war, Jim invited him to come home with him. Since farming on Waldron was out of the question as a money maker, Jim and Prohaska turned their interest to fishing, about the only means of livelihood the island had to offer. So we deliberated on the pros and cons of coming back to the island to stay. My father, of course, was delighted with the idea. I was concerned about Franny's schooling, but Jim said we would cross that bridge when we came to it. I agreed to go if they could arrange to ship my piano. I had taken a few lessons and it helped to while away some lonely hours.

Prohaska (we were calling him *Pro* now) procured an

old hull called the *Orion* and fixed it up for trolling in Alaska. It was into this vessel that we loaded our worldly goods late one December afternoon and sailed off into the stream on a familiar course.

When it became dark, Pro discovered he had forgotten to check the gas tank and there wasn't enough fuel to continue. A fine team they would make, thought I, but they proved themselves. (I suppose anyone could have overlooked such a minor detail during the magnitude of such a move.) They swung the boat in close to the shore of one of the islands and Pro jumped overboard into the icy water and made his way to the nearest gas station. Everything had been closed up for the season, but he managed to rouse someone who supplied us with gas to proceed to Waldron.

We seemed to follow the same old pattern—starting out with a few chickens just for our own use, of course, Pro then thought we really should have a cow, but I quickly demurred, asking, "Just who is going to milk said cow when you guys take off for Alaska?" He answered, "Why, you are, of course!" I seemed to be outnumbered so *Topsy*, the cow, was added to our menage, and who do you suppose learned how to milk?

Next came a few sheep, just to keep the grass whittled down—they would be good for a few lambchops. We could get old ewes for eighteen to twenty dollars a head and lambs brought four to five dollars. Wool didn't amount to much but every little bit counted 'til the fishing venture got underway. In the meantime, Phil and Jim decided to have a new survey made of the place. It had not been done since 1872 and as it was almost impossible to find some of the old markers, Jim hired a surveyor from Orcas and asked Roy Crum and Ralph Wood to help. Their goal was to fence in the whole 160 acres, but first things came first.

Pro worked on the *Orion* and, when our town house sold, we bought the engine and other needed gear and together they let go the lines and sailed off into the morning mists for Elfin Cove and Lituya Bay in Alaska. No sooner had they arrived and had the fishing underway than the Korean War broke out and Prohaska, being a member of the Naval Reserve, was called into active duty. He was assigned to the *U.S.S. Cavalier* as Lt. (j.g.) bound for Tokyo, leaving Jim to carry on alone.

Uneasy lies the head of a man who moors his boat in Cowlitz Bay after the autumn equinox, for if a westerly gale springs up, woe is his! Jim had survived the rigors of Alaskan waters and returned home safely with a few fish. I learned early that fishermen were very cagey about their catch and a *few* could mean any amount from a very poor to a very successful catch. Jim and Denny Huntley, the new mate, had fished quite late at the Cape, always hopeful, but saying they never saw so much water with so few fish.

I thought that our fishing enterprise was about to come to an end when one morning I awoke to the sound of the wind. I instinctively rushed to the window and looked out. The bay was in a boiling lather and the *Orion* which had been moored, was nowhere in sight. I aroused Jim (he was a cool character, never showing his concern) and while he dressed I dashed down the hill to the beach and there was the boat on the shore being lashed by the waves. These westerlies give no warning and are worrisome things. I am sure Jim had been in worse predicaments; he kept his head while I just felt my heart sinking.

First, after dodging the seas, Jim managed to climb aboard, start the engine and look for any damage while I went for help. Stanley Gale came down and as soon as they could float the boat they headed out to Friday Harbor. I guess all I did was pray.

Chapter Ten
Waldron Cauldron
1950-1954

The North Bay shore was becoming quite a settlement, with the "Tibs," Buceys, Dores, and Bucknells all in close proximity to one another in the vicinity of Lyle Beach.

Hazel and Jim Dore had in mind a place for retirement; Jim worked for Boeing and Hazel was a live-wire who wrote the happenings on Waldron for the *Friday Harbor Journal* with humor and bounce. Boyd Bucey also worked for Boeing as a high executive and he and his clever wife, Helen, were laying the groundwork for their future years.

Several young families followed the Taylors and bought property adjoining them that was part of the old Ned Wood estate. Among these were three families from Minnesota who were Quakers, and members of the Religious Society of Friends, and highly dedicated to the cause of peace. The first of these to come were Russ and Millie Thorson with their two small sons, Pier and Rolf; Jack and Lizanne Magraw, with one child, Allison; and Charles and Helen Ludwig with Steve and Meredith.

Roy Bucknell, who before coming to the island had been a freelance photographer, had met Dorothy in Thailand where she had been raised. Her father had been a medical missionary there until they had to flee the country because of uprisings. Roy later did medical photography in Mexico and Seattle. Dorothy was a registered nurse and they had three offspring, Don, Jimmy, and Anore; a fourth child, Susan, was born later. Dorothy gave unstintingly of her time and talent, giving shots to the school children and assisting in the delivery of the

Thorson's third child, Kurt, who was island-born. Then, with her own child strapped to her back she walked across the island to give aid and comfort to our oldest bachelor, Gavin McNaught.

All of them were of different backgrounds, college educated and a little bewildered with wars and rumors of wars, searching to find a way to escape the frustration of the city, trying to find a simpler way of life, working together in harmony and hoping for peace in the world.

Mildred Campbell first came as a guest of the Ludwigs and was drawn to the island, not only for its simple lifestyle and scenic beauty, but also for our fun and frolicking times. She had a background of dramatic art and music, thus contributing much with her lively enthusiasm and zest for life. Her husband, Horace, was a playwright of sorts and a sewing machine expert—repairing some of our rare old relics was right up his alley. The Campbells had two sons, David and Dorn.

I had assisted in the post office before the war, so when Helen Taylor left a vacancy I put in my application and received my appointment as postmaster in February, 1951.

I certainly had my hands full but there is nothing like work to keep one happy, and nothing like dancing to keep one young. The community of young people had really boomed and once again the rafters of Waldronia fairly rang out with the sound of happy feet tripping the light fantastic. This kind of dancing was new to me except what I read about in books; the old fashioned Virginia Reel, the tango, a dance dating back to Babylonian times, the schottische, the polka, and the waltz. We had some good callers for the squares, and the brownies were something else, and when called by Ralph Wood, confusion reigned. I can still hear him in memory, drawling out in his muleskinner's voice, "Ev-rybody dance," (accent on the E) as he maneuvered himself towards the lady of his choice.

We had every kind of *bee* going on—sewing, brush-burning, log-raising, and cider, to mention a few. We organized an Island Improvement Association, working toward better roads, dock-work, and communication. The idea brought us results far beyond our expectations. Showing a willingness to work for ourselves, we won the cooperation of the County Engineer and Commissioners. Not only did we get a fine new dock, but, for the first time, the island had been given a truck for hauling gravel, and the Orcas Island road maintainer, a new Allis-Chalmers, was put at our disposal. John Taylor, who ran the equipment, was like a small boy with a new toy and soon our roads were in better shape than they had ever been.

The Goodriches, John and Gudrun (Goodie, as we called her), were always the life of the party. At that time they had one child, Joe, and they operated the "Isleacres Ranch Resort" in the summer months for several years. Goodie was fun-loving and contributed to all our happy times; she was from Scandinavian stock, as stable as a rock, with no romanticized ideas of life.

John was a character, smart as a whip underneath but forever clowning. Millie Thorson said to him once, "Every day is a masquerade for you, isn't it, John?" For about a couple of years he wrote the *Waldron Cauldron* under the name of "Don Chaotic," which was the wildest, wackiest, and wittiest column of the times, writing of life on the island full of fact, and a sprinkling of fantasy.

The Huntleys, Denny and Jeanne, with their two children were new property owners, having acquired 40 acres at Point Hammond with a view to build and settle. While Prohaska was still in the Navy, Denny fished with Jim on the *Orion* going to Cape Flattery on the Washington coast.

Bob Burn, son of June and Farrar, had married Doris Wernstedt, his childhood playmate. He had served four years in the Navy. Doris was from Portland, Oregon, and had attended the University of Washington (with special courses at the University of Hawaii) and taught school here for one year. Bob and Doris had two small children then, Robin and Mark, and they settled on the island with

Bob having a job with the Alaskan Fisheries.

North Burn was also married and was the American Consulate in Australia with his wife, Babs. North wrote at the time that they were training their first child, Jennifer, to be map conscious; they wanted her to grow up knowing that one of the United States on the map on the wall above her crib was her real homeland. North was extremely patriotic.

Come March, '51, we had a dilly of a storm – 16 inches of snow with freezing temperatures and broken pipes. The county schools were closed but Franny insisted on going, saying it was her last year here and she didn't want to miss any. It took her an hour to break a trail through the new snow. Her teacher, Lizanne Magraw, had not really expected the girls (there were only two of them, the other being Donna Allen) but she left a note on the schoolhouse door, writing that she would be at the cottage if needed.

During the same snow, our sheep began to lamb and one strayed from its mother and had to be fed from a baby bottle. Franny called it "Baby Snooks" and kept it in the barn with her pet chicken which only had one eye. Jim searched through the brush for three miles to rescue a second lamb which he brought into the house for a bottle feeding. He was all for leaving it on the porch, but after seeing the little trail of droppings she left on the kitchen floor, I ruled that one out; she was put in the barn with Topsy's calf and the other little waifs where they coexisted harmoniously. Maybe we could learn a lesson from the animals.

After a full and busy summer, the time came when we were to reach the bridge which Jim said we would have to cross. It was the most difficult and painful decision I was called upon to make – what to do about Franny's schooling? Jim's sister, Stella, who lived in Los Angeles, offered to have her but that seemed to be the end of the earth. She was my only child and I felt I was being robbed of a mother's privilege to be the guiding influence in her daughter's formative years. I was unconsolable. Roy Franklin of Island Sky Ferries swooped down one Sunday morning in his little *Red Hornet* taking Franny and me to Bellingham, where, with heavy hearts, we parted at the railroad station. Franny was going on to Seattle where she would board a plane for Los Angeles.

With several families away, there was still a goodlie companie left to participate in the island's family Thanksgiving Dinner at the schoolhouse. Margaret Severson did a superb job of cleaning, dressing, and roasting one of her 30-pound turkeys. Others matched its goodness with all the traditional trimmings. The school children, under the able direction of their teacher, Irving French, had made little brown turkey place-cards for all of the adults who were seated at one nicely decorated table. The small fry had a separate table which they decorated during the meal in a style of their own.

The feeling of thankfulness for all our blessings was surely expressed in the singing that followed. The question arose, who would play the piano for us, and with a little persuasion, Roy Bucknell, in his quiet, modest way said he would try. It was soon discovered that Roy needed no written notes as the music flowed from his talented fingers, not only hymns and songs but some of his own compositions. My father, Cap Wood, as everyone called him, was delighted that Roy could play some of his old favorites which he sang in the choir as a boy and could still sing at the age of 81.

December started off with a 90 mile an hour gale and our poor old dock, the main lifeline of the island, gave up the ghost. All that remained at the end of the broken ramp was the sign, "YOU USE DOCK AT YOUR OWN RISK." The next day a salvage crew was quickly assembled to recover some of the planking and the several barrels of gasoline and stove oil that had been stored at the shore-end of the ramp.

It is an ill wind, indeed, that blows no good! The

heavy seas caused by this westerly gale had washed out clams from the rocky beach of the bay onto the shingle, making easy pickings for clam fanciers who went down at low water, just popping them into buckets without the aid of shovel or hoe. The beach was also strewn with starfish which had lost their grip. They are a wonderful source of nitrogen for fertilizing strawberries after they have been gathered into the compost pile.

Fortunately a new dock was already under construction; a couple of bents had been dislodged by the pounding of the seas, but with a few days' work it was put to rights and ready for the *Bobbie B* and the new mail contractor, Bob Murray.

By this time, Prohaska had been released from active duty in the Navy and he and Jim worked feverishly to make ready the *Orion* for the fishing season. Early in May they took off for Seattle to obtain some last minute equipment and freight for the island. They were forced by bad weather to leave their berth at Lake Union, to find shelter, and, thought Jim, what a better place to go than Pier 28 where all the big ships dock. The Olympic Steamship Company, for whom Jim had sailed for several years as skipper, greeted them with open arms. The *Orion* was the guest for the night, given all the dockside services, lights, watchmen, and longshoremen, while Jim and Pro went on their merry way to see the bright lights of the city. They returned the next day, loaded to the gunnels, with lumber dragging in the water, at which, I'm sure, Lloyds of London would have raised a disapproving eyebrow.

There were rumors of a troller's strike which dampened their spirits somewhat so they welcomed the little diversion that the Waldron community had planned as a farewell party for them. With renewed eagerness they soon set sail once again for the Alaskan fishing ground and Elfin Cove.

My duties at the post office increased with the coming of the summer crowds, and, with the men away I found that milking two cows along with my other chores was rather a burden, so I decided to farm out Topsy for the summer. Mrs. Dore welcomed the idea of having fresh milk and cream, but I was not so sure of her husband, Jim.

Poor Topsy, you could hear her loud lamentations all over the island. She was blind in one eye. Her previous owner in a fit of anger had hit her over the head with a chain, and maybe she thought she was being taken back to her cruel taskmaster. First off, Topsy was in disgrace; Hazel may have been able to forgive her for eating up her choice lilies, but for getting rough with Jim, it was doubtful. Jim nursed some pretty sore ribs after a little encounter with bossy. Dorothy, our competent nurse, came to the rescue taping him up and giving the necessary first aid treatment.

I really did enjoy my job as postmaster. The bookkeeping was simple: it included money orders, registration, insurance and sometimes customs besides hand stamping, sorting, and distributing the mail. I was practically my own boss and my patrons never made any undue demands on me, mostly coming to do their mailing at boat-time. I liked the contact with people and it was a good place to gather news for the paper, which I wrote from time to time.

The spring was full of surprises, with visits from the family. First my sister, Geva, came and then Franny. Franny's letters had not prepared me for the vital change in her: the transition from a bewildered little girl in pigtails to a self-composed, blossoming young lady was phenomenal. At first she was homesick, she wasn't used to the Los Angeles heat, but she soon adjusted, doing well in school and receiving three special awards. Stella and Los Angeles had been good for her, but she was glad to be back in Washington where everything was so cool and green and the trees so beautiful.

In spite of the gravity of the times, folks responded with infectious spontaneity to our get-togethers, whether a beach picnic, a dance or just singing around the piano. Having the piano was a source of great pleasure over the years. One of these doings was the beginning of what John Goodrich called "The Chant and Chowder Society" – he claimed that those who could not sing could clam up. We were beginning to discover all kinds of little things about each other and the bond of friendship grew.

We discovered that John had a fine tenor voice. Roy Bucknell discovered that I could reach a high G. Dorothy had a lovely, trained voice, Mildred a delicately sweet one and Chuck Ludwig was a bass, so we formed a quartet with Dorothy conducting and Goodie accompanying us on the piano. We practiced hard and in time we offered our little musical contribution at house parties and school happenings.

We discovered that Chuck could play the violin and as my father could play the harmonica and accordion, they would spell off the old phonograph at the dances, which were becoming increasingly popular.

Dad was always happy on these occasions and he loved to dance. My sister, Mabel, and brother Frank, had joined the "Woodpile," and Stella and a friend came up from Los Angeles to take Franny back to school. We were having a picnic on the beach with the others and our fire served as a beacon at sundown to welcome home the fishermen, Jim and Pro, on the *Orion*. They had cut short their fishing activities to enable Pro to take his examination for the Captain's license, "Oceans Unlimited." This he obtained in October with the extra distinction of being the youngest man on record at the Seattle Steamship Inspector's office to receive this grade of license.

After Pro and Franny left, Jim settled down to farming again, building more fence and gathering in the harvest of apples. There were several *bees* going on and there was heap big smoke when we gathered at Squire and Lou Gale's place. We made fun out of work while swinging axes, dragging brush and trees, feeding them to the flames. Happy voices could be heard singing, "Water boy, where are you hiding?" as we warmed up to the job.

It was October and the days were golden; appetites were whetted with honest toil. Times like these, helping our neighbors and being satisfied with simple joys, make for peace and contentment.

We followed up with another bee at the Frenches. Irving had retired from his high school teaching in Bellingham and Marjorie from her job in the post office, where she had worked for many years. The same spirit had prevailed as we tore through blackberry vines, entangled hardhack, scotch broom, and wild gooseberry. We looked like attendants of Hades with pitchforks and flame throwers as we fed the offending growth to the fiery furnace.

The little Christmas programs at the schoolhouse were always a source of delight; the children were so imaginative and original. On one occasion, Sandra Taylor and Anore Bucknell, who had the lead roles, were indisposed by the flu, so their mothers, Helen and Dorothy, substituted for them in a one-act play, adding a touch of humor to the grim realities of a pioneer's Christmas a hundred years ago. No turkey with all the trimmings for them; not even a postage stamp for twelve cents due on a long-awaited letter from home; and only one paper to read—the *Friday Harbor Journal*.

How great was their joy when a neighbor arrived with some fresh venison and father came back with shoes, muslin, some tea, and sugar. Times may change, but the spirit of Christmas, never. The children soon forgot their temporary hardships as they set about distributing gifts from underneath the beautiful tree to all present. No matter how poor we are we have a gift within us to give and share.

It was a clear and moonlight night and the Goodriches and Burns, accompanied by the Thorsons, raised their voices on high with carols. Gathering by twos and threes, they went to each and every house. Some who had already retired thought they had left their radio on and others thought they were dreaming, but everyone entered into the spirit of the evening.

Once again it became the parting of the ways for me and my mate—on December 20th, Roy Franklin dropped a message from his plane from the Olympic Steamship Company. It was tied in a rag and weighted with a rock which hit the woodshed roof, and within the hour Jim had his gear packed and was winging his way to Seattle to join a ship bound for San Francisco.

He was gone for ten months this time, having made two trips coast-wise and four trips to foreign ports, taking supplies during the Korean War. On several occasions the ship's port of call had been the city of New York, giving Jim an opportunity to see his brother, Phil, where together they had taken in a few night spots and places of interest.

Phil at the time was working for the firm of Andrews and Clark as chief designer. He and his associates were designing the underpasses that were to divert traffic from the United Nations' building.

When Jim's ship, the *Rock Springs Victory*, was put into mothballs, he was due for a vacation, so I flew to San Francisco to meet him and we came home together.

Dr. William Cook and his wife, Beatrice, of *Till Fish Do Us Part* and *More Fish To Fry* fame, became our very good friends. They had bought the old Doucette place on the northeast shore of the island and Bill loved to fish around Waldron. While Bill was fishing, Bea and I would go blackberrying. We never had to go very far in those days and I would serve the berries with heavy cream.

I remember one time when Dr. Bill and Bea had come to Waldron arriving simultaneously with the *Chickawana*, and while the islanders were gathered on the dock they took advantage of a little medical advice from the doctor, airing out their ailments. It was an impromptu free clinic. Bill had checked and put on a fresh bandage to my injured thumb. I had a little accident the week before as I was chopping cedar kindling while in a state of high elation. I had received a letter from Jim with four one-hundred dollar money orders enclosed. I had never seen so much money, not even in the post office, and to think it was our very own. I must have overreacted on the chopping block, almost severing the end of my thumb. While I endeavored to stem the flow of blood, Franny reached for the bandage. We made our way to the Jones' and across the island to Frank Graignic who took me in his little open putt-putt to Friday Harbor where I received medical help and nine stitches.

It was through Bea's efforts that we opened our first library, which we called the *Sally Ployart Island Library* after the lady from Frederick & Nelson's book department who so kindly supplied us with a fine selection of advanced copies of books for all ages. They included *Light on the Island*, a story of Patos Lighthouse by Helene Glidden, and *The Glorious Three*, a novel of early homesteaders with part of its plot centered on Waldron and written by June Wetherel. We invited others to join us and it became a circulating island project. We were favored with books from Ann Sterling of KJR, Seattle, and Dr. Guthrie of Shaw. We kept them at the post office building, starting with a couple of orange crates and working up to several well-filled shelves.

Russ and Millie Thorson at the time were occupying the 75 year-old log cabin on the now Cook's property, and we had our first beach workout party there in February with a minus tide about seven in the evening, just right for a clam dig. Most of our affairs were impromptu and a merry crowd came with buckets, shovels and hoes and set out to Point Hammond. The beach was soon dotted with lantern lights as little groups bent over a likely spot. Some hit the jackpot while others had to dig deep and wide to find the elusive, squirting bivalves.

The stars seemed to shine with an extra brightness and the lights from the mainland and Saturna Lighthouse twinkled in the calm, clear night. When our backs felt as though we had overturned half the beach, we wandered back to the cabin where preparations were underway for a big clam chowder feed, which my father called low-tide soup. The evening was spent around a cozy fire singing and such. We followed up with a Valentine candlelight party at the post office—firelight, too—and the little glowworm glimmered as we danced to its music. (Doesn't that sound romantic?)

With the prospects of Jim having steady employment, we sold our interest in the troller, *Orion*, to Don Prohaska who continued to fish for a while before making a trip to see his parents and to earn a bachelor's degree in Marine Science.

I felt very proud of myself after going to the mainland and buying a good Chevrolet pickup and chain saw. This made things easier all around. Franny had brought her friend, Lani, home from Los Angeles and the two girls kept things lively all summer; Franny learned how to drive the vehicles. Billy Chevalier was home on shore leave from the Navy. He had graduated from Friday Harbor High School, then enlisted. After two years of training he received orders for overseas duty serving on the U. S. S. *Orleck* during the Korean War.

My brother, Charles, and his son, Bobby, came that summer, their first visit since they had left the island 13 years earlier. The house was bulging at the seams with most of the family represented: my sister, Marian, and son, Jimmy; brother, Frank; Geva and George; and Madge and Harold. There was never a dull moment and my father was very happy to join in all the fun—dancing, fishing, picnics, and beachcombing.

The little cottontail rabbits were multiplying so rapidly they were becoming a pest in the garden. Jim bought me a .22 rifle and instructed me on how to use and handle it. I became quite adept shooting at long distances. They were good eating after being dressed and refrigerated and there were many little families who enjoyed them.

My dad fancied himself as sort of a Pied Piper to rid the island of rabbits and was working on a new improved trap. He was thus inspired when his first model, which heretofore only attracted earwigs, trapped seven rabbits and Roy Crum's cat within a week.

Ice skating is certainly a novelty in this usually mild climate, but almost everyone seemed ready with skates when Ralph Wood's pond froze over. I wasn't there, I had to have wheels on mine, but from all reports it was great fun, with bonfires and torches and even music for waltzing for the advanced, and numerous spills for the beginners. Helen Ludwig supplied hot food and coffee from her kitchen.

A party wouldn't be complete without the town clown and he obliged with some fancy figures that landed him on the wrong side of the ice. As usual he took it cooly. The instigator of the affair, Mark Hayes, wound up the evening with a sprained knee and you may be sure there were plenty of other tender spots. With the exception of Mark, who presented his skates to Irving French for the remainder of the season, everyone was ready for more skating the next day at Margaret Severson's. Goodie Goodrich called such times our "Ice Follicles."

In the wee small hours, the Burns were having their own private party with the arrival of their third bairn, Cameron. They had every reason to be the proud parents of this new baby boy; having no telephones or doctors on the island, we had to anticipate emergencies and they were ready for this one. Bob was confident and knew what was expected of him, and Doe was happy and unafraid to have her son at home as nature intended.

There were several changes in the community as the days wore on. Jim was called back into ships' business and put in charge of loading grain storage ships in Seattle and Portland. Irving French was to retire from his teaching at the island's school. His son, Don, was to embark on his career as a pharmacist; he had won a scholarship and was to leave in the fall for Ann Arbor, Michigan, to study for a

Ph.D. at the University.

A toot of his whistle and a lowering of the flag (just a fun gesture) marked the end of Walt Sutherland's term of contract for carrying mail on the M. V. Macard. To commemorate the occasion, all the islanders planned a pot-luck lunch at the post office to show their appreciation for his fine, friendly, service to the island and to bid him farewell. We then welcomed Ed Martel, skipper of the Denny M, who was to be our next mail carrier. The contracts were usually for a four-year period.

Things were bustling at the schoolhouse when the islanders all pitched in for a clean-up bee. The women washed windows and painted the inside walls while the men made necessary repairs on the outside. Thus, everything was in ship-shape order for our next school teacher, Mildred Campbell, who had moved onto her little acreage with her boys David and Dorn (boosting the school enrollment to about fourteen).

The beginnings of an exodus started when Jim and Hazel Dore left the island for Seattle. Jim was in very poor health and the winters were hard for them both. It saddened us to see them leave and we missed Hazel's bubbling personality and her cheerful, little earfuls in the Journal. Ray and Mary Tiberghien would also leave in the fall, but we could always count on them to return in due season, like harbingers of spring, when the crocuses were in bloom.

When the crickets started to chirp and the geese had flown south, Lou Gale, now the grandmother of six, would leave the silence and serenity of the island to join her family, Peggy and Joe Heider, and the hustle and bustle of Seattle and their six little live wires; Barbara Lou, Loretta, John, Larry, Mike, and Edward. As most grandmothers do, she delighted in it.

Since we had sold off all of our livestock life became easier, giving me the freedom to make an occasional trip off the island. Then Jim received his next call to the waterfront, I accompanied him to Seattle. He was assigned to the *Flemish Knot* as Master, sailing to the Arctic, taking part in the establishment and movement of supplies for the Distant Early Warning Radar Station (DEW-Line), which was to take him 1600 miles east of Pt. Barrow and within 900 miles of the North Pole. The vast sea movement of men and materials on a huge scale in the dead of winter, and the start of construction despite frigid temperatures, blizzards, and rugged locations, was unprecedented in either military or civilian operations in arctic North America. Construction of the DEW-Line was expected to give American cities four to six hours warning of a bombing attack across the Polar region.

In preparation for the trip, the ship's bow and hull plates were reinforced and strengthened so that the ice floes could be bucked in safety. Sailing in the ice in uncharted waters was a whole new ball game in which ordinary rules of seamanship did not always apply. Underwater growlers (submerged icebergs) were a particular menace. Jim's ship had the misfortune of running into one which made quite a hole in her hull. The trip lasted about three months, during which time Jim had some hair-raising experiences.

Albert Severson, another of our seven-seas sailor men, was also engaged in Operation DEW-Line, sailing from the east coast on a naval vessel going by the way of St. Lawrence to the land of the blue-nose mermaids and midnight sun, the Aurora Borealis, and willawaws. In 1957, Canada's patrol ship *Labrador* discovered the fabled Northwest Passage in Bellot Strait while charting a deep water, relatively ice-free passage from the Atlantic to the Pacific, across the top of North America. The strait was the key link in a route to provide an escape to the Atlantic, for DEW-Line ships in the event any unpredictable movements of the Arctic ice pack should block the normal exit passage to the Pacific.

After I had said goodbye to my sailor man I continued

my trek down to Los Angeles for Franny's high school graduation and in due time we were homeward bound.

The Weaver family, Bob and Mary, with Josie, Nellie, Andy, and Chris, first came to Waldron on an experimental basis for about a year. They were from Goshen, Indiana, where they had a farm, chickens, and a garden. Among other things, Bob and his brother-in-law, Dr. Eigsti, were absorbed in genetics, chromosomes, and tetraploids in the process of producing a seedless watermelon, which they eventually perfected.

They were a talented and very musical family with fine natural voices and Mary was another like Roy Bucknell, whose piano music had that certain charm. They could play anything from Bach to Boogie, much to the delight of us all. They added quality to our quartet and it had been the beginning of another beautiful friendship. They returned to Indiana having already succumbed to the island's magic and left their indelible mark on us all. As Ethan Allen used to say, anyone spending even a day on Waldron would yearn to return another day.

After six years of trying to make a success out of their business venture, Isleacres Ranch Resort, the Goodriches came to the conclusion they weren't making any money. Their family had increased with the birth of another boy, Paul, and Goodie had her hands full with John commuting. They sold the ranch to Otto Mittelstadt who had a mortuary business in Seattle and property on Orcas. John stayed on for a year as manager while it was changed over to the Black Angus Farm. The new owner had transported these prize animals from his place on Orcas.

John and Goodie moved to Seattle where John said it was easier to find a job than find a house to rent; this jolly, lively, yet serious couple left a gaping hole in the community but we were to see them often. Goodie used to say when the Balm of Gilead started to waft over the sandflats she would have a yearning to return. They were our lifelong friends.

I wasn't too well acquainted with the Mittelstadts, but one incident stands out in my memory. The day was turning to dusk and I was settling down for a quiet evening when there was a knock on the door. It was Otto, the friendly undertaker, who said in his subdued and most professional voice, "Mrs. Lovering, I have your husband here." With a sinking feeling I expected to see the pine box follow, but it was Jim on crutches coming slowly up the path, his leg in a cast. He had tripped over a chain on the deck of his ship and had fallen, breaking his ankle. He was at home for about six weeks.

Chapter Eleven
Old-Time Bachelors

It was quite common in early times for a bachelor to advertise for a wife. Charlie Fahlstrom did just that. He built a fine, frame house for the occasion of this bride-to-be's coming but their union did not last; his mail-order matron was soon to leave him. Years later there was a shroud of mystery concerning his death. He had been in ill health and had gone to the mainland to see a doctor and to make arrangements to stay awhile at a nursing home where he signed over all his worldly property to the owners. A few days later we received word that he was dead and his remains cremated and buried. Since he was Norwegian, the Norwegian consul looked into the case but was unable to prove anything irregular. Charles had been a good neighbor and a hard worker. He will be long remembered, as the county road running through his place is to this day called Charlie Fahlstrom's Road.

This same year, 1953, we lost another of our dear old bachelors; Gavin McNaught passed away at the age of 83. I used to be confused when he said he was a Scot, his having been born in the County Tipperary and all; he and his brothers sure had a bit o' the wit of the Irish. The McNaughts came from a family of seven boys (most of whom were six-footers), and two girls. Gavin came to Waldron in 1925 with his brother Jim, and together they lived a frugal and kindly life on their well-ordered farm which had formerly been the Rayhorst's place. Ten years later their brother, Fred, joined them. He was used to vast, wide open spaces and at one time had managed a 30,000 acre sheep ranch in New Zealand, where he wouldn't see a soul for weeks at a time. He would say that the only place he was lonely was the big city.

I met Fred one day at the airfield and thinking it was news I was after, he said, "Tell them we haven't had any excitement since we ate our last missionary." It was the first time in 17 years that he made a trip off the island.

In the course of time it was necessary for Fred to have both of this legs amputated and when he returned from a three months' stay at the hospital this doughty, old "Scot" smiled courageously as he was lifted from the plane saying, "Well, I made it." He had never given up hope of returning to his cabin and to seeing his friends, the birds, and little creatures. He learned to manipulate himself in and out of his bed into his wheelchair and out to his woodpile; he used more ropes and pulleys than a full-rigged ship, and from his wheelchair he made his own fires, cooked his simple meals, and split his stovewood. The islanders watched over him, attending to his other needs, bringing him water and sawing his wood.

It takes a lot of different people to make up the world and Walter, another brother who came to stay with Fred, was quite the opposite. He was also in his eighties and in his youth had led a gay and colorful life; he still had a twinkle in his eye and the sweetest smile when he would look at the ladies saying, "Yoorr an aingel." He loved to tell of the days when he served in the Queen's Royal Guard at Windsor Castle, having charge of the young Duke, putting him up on a stand to see a football game, taking part in the Queen's Jubilee in 1900, going to balls and dances and even tipping a wee drappie with the Tsar of Russia and Edward when he was the Prince of Wales.

Walter had a varied career, having at one time been a rancher in Canada and a landscape architect in Los Gatos, California. He had all kinds of plans for landscaping Fred's place, but his time came sooner than expected and in a few years he was, no doubt, shaking hands with angels. He was buried beside his brothers in our secluded little cemetery.

Fred continued to live alone and his door was always open to his friends and the wasps which he called mason bees or mud daubers which built their nests in the dark corners of his cabin. He also liked to quote poetry and offered me these few words of wisdom, "We'll hae misfortune great and sma, but aye a heart to aboon them all." I always came away from these little visits having learned something and with a feeling of humility. He was so gentle with the little rabbits which he fed with apple peelings at his doorstep and he had a system of telling the time of day by the sun's shadow on the floor.

In spite of Fred's chiding and scolding I think he secretly enjoyed being mentioned and quoted in my column. He was quite concerned one time because I got his remedies and maladies mixed up. He claimed it was all our fancy eating which accounted for most of our ills, but he had a panacea that would cure most everything. He didn't want to put Dr. Heath out of business, but if anyone was willing to try it he wanted them to have the correct dosage for the right malady. For colds or influenza, swallow one or two drops of eucalyptus oil and spirits of camphor. For cuts and abrasions, use coal oil; just pour it on and rub it in.

Fred believed that a meteor had fallen on Waldron. He told of having seen a brilliant light flash followed by a thud. Years later Rolf Thorson blazed a trail to the likely spot and discovered an indentation about 40 feet across and very deep. One theory was that, if a meteor had fallen, it must still be there because it made such a deep hole. Another theory was, could the hole be hand-made, and for what purpose?

Fred lived until he was 96, and he was laid to rest alongside his three brothers. Rolf Thorson wrote these few sensitive lines, "It happens every day, but for most, just once. Thirty-six summers on the island till early spring of '71, waiting for the Master. The spark of life departed, a flash in the void, to take form again within the womb of Mother Nature. The silken sounds of rain on rain wash away the tracks."

Roy Crum, our one-time postmaster and storekeeper, needs no further introduction. His self-sufficiency and industry benefitted us all, and his many humorous anecdotes added a special flavor to island life. His last endeavor was to build a scow which he planned for his final journey. He laid down his tools in June of '55, and after a simple island ceremony his remains were returned to the earth which he loved, and as he would so often say, "That's true, too."

Ralph Wood was a simple soul, a veteran of W.W.I., and he loved kids and cats. When he wasn't building up his wood pile he was out fishing at the reef, supplying his neighbors with ling and rock cod.

Ralph's roots went pretty deep. He didn't believe in all this running around and his trips were limited to a run over to Orcas to buy ice cream and candy for the kids. He had innumerable cats. He also served as an island barometer, letting his hair grow during the winter primarily to keep his ears warm, but when he cut it in the springtime you could go ahead and plant your garden. He was pretty reliable, not easily taken in by all the early murmurings of spring.

Ralph had been walking to the post office for many a long year and ran a sort of rural, free delivery service, picking up the mail for his neighbors. We shook our heads and our serenity was shaken when he announced one day that he was tired of walking and that he was going to buy a car. He thought it would be a cinch to learn to drive and he had a system all worked out. He knew how to go ahead and how to back up but he found it a little different than driving a team of horses; his first mishap was to run over a rock and tear off the drain plug to the oil pan. Ralph was soon hoofing it again.

His solo flights into the automotive world were costly; as a driving tyro he developed the common failing of riding the clutch, so back went his Plymouth convertible into dry dock for new parts. This in no way dampened his spirits, and when his sister, Gertrude Collins, came for a visit he would drive her all around the island as pleased as Punch but he could not understand why it wouldn't go any faster than it did. He had yet to learn that brakes were to be released when the car was in motion, so back went the turquoise fluid-drive into Corky's Repair.

Ralph finally went to live with his sister, Gertrude, in Bellingham. Bachelors at least seem to have one advantage over married men; they all live to a ripe old age. At least our island variety did.

Mark Hayes was another bachelor who played a significant role in the Waldron story. He didn't exactly come under the heading of *Old-Time Bachelors* but he was definitely a loner, except for his dog, Babe, who was his constant companion.

Jim and I had good reason to be very grateful to Babe one time. Franny had taken a hike with her dogs, Belle and Half-Hitch, on the mountain. She loosened some logs on the way back which rolled down the hill knocking her over and pinning her legs down. She cried for help and it was Babe who heard her cries, Babe pricked her ears and started to whimper, and Mark, sensing that she was alarmed about something, followed her until he too could hear Franny. Mark then came for Jim and between them they carried her down the steep descent. Franny had been badly bruised, but no bones were broken.

When Babe died, Mark made a special enclosure for her, planting a young dogwood tree over the spot. I believe it is still living.

In 1960, Mark had a hankering for his gold mining diggin's and to explore them thar hills. He worked for a while in Alaska, but returned to Bellingham after a bad fall. Some of his friends found him there alone without family. He died in 1977, and his remains were brought to Waldron where a service was held in his memory; and a new grave appeared under the dogwood trees. When Mark was still living in our old tumble-down shack he adopted the address *711 Hawthorne Lane* after he had planted and cared for Phil's avenue of trees. And below this sign on his door he added, "You can't have style and comfort, too." This is the sign that now marks his grave.

Chapter Twelve
Troubled Waters
1956-1957

Franny knew from the beginning that college life was not for her. She argued that Marge and Betty Chevalier didn't have college educations and they were doing fine, but just for my sake and the family's she consented to try for a while and went to Western Washington College in Bellingham for a few semesters, after which she changed to a College of Commerce and secretarial training. I was glad to have her close to home as she was to be a great comfort to me during the ensuing months.

She was then dating Billy Chevalier, her childhood idol, and everything seemed to be smooth sailing until one day they had a lover's quarrel. Franny was employed as a stenographer. While taking dictation at the MacMaster's Sign Company one day, a gas jet which was burning nearby exploded and caught her clothing on fire. Her condition was not serious, but very painful and she was hospitalized. During her stay there Billy kept his silence and distance. Franny was deeply hurt.

My father at this time was 85 and failing. It was necessary for him to go to Bellingham Hospital for tests and subsequent surgery. I remember how he braced himself, squaring his shoulders and never looking back as we made our way to the waiting plane. This was his first and last ride in the air. He had tucked away some of his sailing ship pictures and poems to show to the nurses; he loved an audience when he could talk about one of his favorite subjects. He never returned to his beloved island. For six months the merciless fingers of cancer spread and took their toll of body and soul.

To add to our distress news came of the death of my

brother, Frank. There had been an accident at sea; he was a chief mate for the Matson Steamship Co. He was inspecting the cargo holds when the Captain gave an order for a sudden change of course that threw Frank off balance. He fell 50 feet to his death. There had been something highly irregular about the incident, it seemed to me, but no charges were brought forth.

My father kept asking me, "What has become of my son, Frank? Strange he has not written." When I hesitated and, noticing my discomfort, he asked, "Is he dead?" When I told him he said, "I have sensed it all along."

These valiant voyagers of the sea seem to be a special breed of men. Through it all my father never lost his awareness and was ready to cross the bar when his time came. He died on his 86th birthday, the 26th of June, 1956, so once again our families and friends gathered for services and my father was laid to rest by the side of my mother. He used to say that the island was about as close to heaven as he ever expected to get.

During Dad's last days, Jim was in the Arctic region waging war with violent north winds, willawaws, and ice floes that threatened to force his ship ashore. Despite all these worrisome things, these were happier times and we called them the Fabulous Fifties. As they gradually came to an end the old gang started to break up. Although their paths would lead them in various directions they all had one thing in common; that was a wish to return to Waldron on vacation or possibly retire here. They had given something of themselves to enrich the bond of friendship which continued over the years.

The Taylors were gone; the Bucknells moved to Seattle, each contributing their bit to society, Roy in the field of medical photography and Dorothy furthering her nursing career.

Russ Thorson found employment in Bellingham, and a little eight-acre farm with a stream running through, an ideal place to raise their boys, Peer, Rolf, Joel, Kurt, and

Nils. When the sixth one, Stennar, came, someone asked Russ if the new baby was a boy and he asked in return, "Is there any other kind?"

Chuck and Helen Ludwig had gone their separate ways. Helen's sympathetic and generous nature was to lead her into several channels, nursing the sick, and caring for and teaching art to disturbed children.

Chuck was attending the University of Washington working toward a doctor's degree in organic chemistry. During this time he compiled and wrote *A Brief History of Waldron*, which added to his credits. Mildred Campbell, after her two years of teaching on the island, became the new Mrs. Charles H. Ludwig and was in Seattle teaching 26 lively, little first-graders at Loyal Heights Elementary School.

Bob Burn, with his family of four, moved to Seattle and worked as a carpenter. Doe's forte was drawing, an artist in her field of illustration which she doggedly pursued and which was to win her renown for her books and illustrations. Their years away from Waldron were brief.

The Magraws were pretty well settled with four little girls to their credit. They had remodeled their 75 year-old cabin and had built a fine, large, stone fireplace to enhance its beauty and comfort. Jack was a manufacturer's representative and traveled a lot; we used to call him our low-pressure salesman; he would shake his head and say everything was hectic and business was so "terrible good." He received many recognitions from his company as Salesman of the Year. Lizanne was interested in the school and served as Clerk of the Board for several years before she became the teacher herself. Jack and Lizanne were still very active in the work of the Religious Society of Friends and over the years had invited college students from all over the world to visit, enjoy the island, and share their thoughts and opinions with us.

I remember one sunny Sunday we were enjoying a beach picnic and a young man from Java, who wore a wet towel around his head and complained of the sun, said it made him so very dark. That must have been one of our *Banana Belt* days.

Lizanne had majored in home economics and she was a whiz in the kitchen and a gracious hostess. The Magraw's place was our favorite stomping ground for cider bees, and it was so lovely to gather there in the fall when the leaves of the Lombardy poplars would turn a delicate, pale yellow gold, standing out in such contrast against the deep blue of the sky and the dark evergreens. These tall, stately trees had been planted over half a century ago, as were the trees from which we gathered so many beautiful apples. Cider bees were becoming a tradition on Waldron, there seemed at that time to be an unlimited supply of Gravensteins, Bellflowers, Kings, Yellow Transparents, Roman Beauties, and several unknown varieties.

The McDonalds, Norman and Alice, were from Newburyport, Massachusetts, and were drawn to the island because of its quiet beauty. Norman had retired from the sea and loved the loneliness of life by and on the water. At the age of 72, he wrote his first book called *The Song of the Axe*, and thought the life on the island would be ideal. Norman had spent boyhood on Orcas; his father had a grocery store at Olga. Island life was nothing new to Alice for she had lived on Lummi Island years before she went back east; so the tides and the woodlands beckoned them to return. They occupied the old Mae Doucette cabin which was now owned by Dr. and Mrs. William Cook.

Someone writing about Waldron said that we had no this or no that and no entertainment of any kind. If they meant no movies or TV, then they were right, but we never lacked entertainment.

Times and photography were continually changing; it hadn't been too long ago that when one brought out the family album it was a sure sign it was time to leave, now it is the fashionable host who invites you to see his pictures. And so, on Waldron, people would gather for a slide show.

Over the years I had become a camera buff and had a fine collection of colored slides and, since Jim had wired our meeting house, bringing electric current from our home generator, on several occasions we put on a show for the island.

I personally operated the projector and explained the subject which was all part of the fun. If I didn't have it out of focus, it was off the screen or upside down, but the pictures would eventually settle down and zero in. I was partial to sunsets and flowers and shady lanes but I also had a collection of slides of our social affairs—Fourth of July picnics, school graduations, and Christmas programs, all in the review. We even had some slides of the ships in the ice floes that Jim had taken while in the Arctic.

If we wanted a live show, nature was always willing to oblige in season—during a nor'wester you could watch the turmoil of the sea and gulls pitting their strength against the wind, the patterned flight of the geese coming or going, and the *Ballet of the Birds* as Mildred would call it as they congregated at the water's edge. When a snow had fallen, it was fun to watch the antics of the fat, saucy robins who seemed to be hopping mad, pecking at the fallen apples, while the towhees made soundings in the frozen earth. On occasion, the northern lights put on a spectacular show.

Nature could also be exasperatingly cruel and Captain Jim, who had made his last voyage to the Arctic in 1957, said he never again wanted to come so close to losing his ship. It had been a grueling and tortuous trip. He was mighty glad to come home for Christmas, his first in three years. The following is a copy of my newspaper article which describes what happened:

Captain Jim Lovering Has Exciting Experience

Captain Jim Lovering of Waldron Island is home on vacation after successfully completing his mission in the Arctic Region at the top of the world.

Jim reports that the ice conditions in the Cana- dian Arctic were the worst that he had yet encountered with the persistent Northwest winds bringing down fresh polar ice faster than it could melt. On one particular morning this same Northwest wind, blowing between 20 and 45 miles an hour, brought in a large field of ice. A giant floe of about three acres in extent and four to five feet thick lodged across the bow of Jim's ship, the *Flemish Knot*, which was anchored and discharging cargo at one of the DEW-line sites.

The floe dragged the ship toward the beach. With engines going full ahead, an attempt was made to heave up the anchor, but the pressure was so great that the chain parted and the anchor was lost. Then they were able to back a few feet and ramming the ice full speed ahead were able eventually to break their way through the ice floe.

The unit Commodore dispatched a large Navy tug to assist the *Flemish Knot*, and it took them five hours to come the five miles to reach her. For the next sixteen hours both vessels fought a long and weary battle with the ice. During this time the tug lost one propeller and seriously damaged her rudder, and was finally given orders to abandon the *Flemish Knot* and attempt to save herself.

It is hard for some of us to conceive the tremendous responsibility and deep feeling the captain has for his ship. When Jim was asked if the crew panicked, and was questioned about fighting for his life, he explained that he was not fighting for his life but was fighting for his ship; he and his crew would have walked ashore.

When there was nothing more that could be done Jim went below and had another cup of coffee. Then the wind died down, relieving the pressure, thus enabling them to proceed.

The episode with the *Flemish Knot* breaking ice for the Navy tug which had come to help her and with the exception of a few dents and wrinkles in her sides, the *Flemish Knot* came through undamaged.

The coming of the *Christmas Ship* was fast becoming a tradition among the islands; we would all await its arrival at the dock with anticipation. We were touched by this symbol of Christmas, the gaily lighted tree, music wafting across the waters, and the friendliness of jolly old St. Nick and his helpers who brought gifts of candy and oranges to the bright-eyed youngsters. It was always an adventure for the children who live so far from the big stores, and what fun it was to snap their picture with Santa. There were many times that it had been so stormy that even the stouthearted crew of the *Discovery* wouldn't venture across the turbulent waters of Boundary Bay to come from Pender Island. Nevertheless, the spirit of Christmas which they were bringing and which not storm could prevent, would reach its destination. The gifts would arrive later by plane and "Santa" Franklin would buzz his helper, Mark "Claus," and he in turn would distribute them around the island.

Christmas was always a very special time on Waldron but to have Jim home with me to share its joy was an extra special premium. Jim was choosy about his tree, and we would travel what seemed miles from one likely copse to the next wooded knoll, traipsing and tripping in the blackberry vines. If they grew too dense, the trees were spindly and tall; if out in the wind, they would be misshapen; the just right spots are open but protected and it was sheer enchantment to listen to the twit-twit of the birds as we trod on the deep carpet of mosses, and *oh!* how sweet the stillness.

The urgency of Christmas was made manifest by the increased tempo at the post office—people sending trees all wrapped up like mummies, ready to release their fragrance in one nostalgic wave over the recipient; and boxes containing the essence of Waldron, wreaths of sweet-smelling firs and cedar with cones, snowberries, and Oregon grape; the piles of packages coming and going. One year there had been a tree labeled, "To: Mrs. John Goodrich," from "Mrs. Crazy Neighbor," but with no address. It reached its destination. Don Chaotic's memory would linger on.

Chapter Thirteen
Ebb and Flow
1958-1959

Our island interlude was short and sweet and came to an end when Jim was called back to sea. For the next two years he was to sail coast-wise which would enable us to have more time together at home and in the different ports. He left on New Year's Eve for Seattle.

With January comes the pause that refreshes, time to reflect upon the joys of the holiday season and to thumb through the colorful seed catalogues with their promise of big and better begonias, petunias, and tomatoes.

That nature will repeat its miracle of the seasons is one thing we can be reasonably sure of in this changing world. The first signs of renewed life in the cold, sleepy earth were all about us as the snowdrops pushed up their dainty bowed heads and the early crocuses brought a dash of color to the gardens. The first pussy willows, sprays of sopololly with their tiny chartreuse blossoms and bronze leaves brightening a bouquet, the bleating of little lambs, and that buoyant feeling of eagerness to clear last year's cornstalks were all forerunners of spring.

February started off with a bang when the one-armed bandit, Miss Elsie Scott, invaded the island to do a little shooting. Despite the fact that her arm was in a sling because of an injury, Miss Scott came to the island when really only angels should fly. Miss Scott spent her time and energies in service to the sick and needy, bringing health education to the island. We were grateful to her for her faithful consideration of Waldron, making and missing flights in all kinds of weather in our behalf. It was all part of her tireless work and love for humanity.

Bob Schoen's little ferry the, *Nordland,* played a significant role in our transportation needs and its arrival was always an event. A couple of toots on her whistle would bring folks scurrying down to the dock to see who and what she was bringing. There was usually a race with the changing tide and a feverish haste to land the gas and oil, tools, groceries, cars, trucks, tractors, household goods, bicycles, dogs, livestock, and even the proverbial kitchen sink.

I often wondered how Noah ever managed to cram all those animals into the ark. When we would dispose of our animals and try to load them onto the ferry, it would be a tug-of-war with plenty of tail-twistin'. Wrestling a bull, or a cow and her calf aboard ended in a tie-up and sit-down strike! Lizanne let out a big sigh of relief when her sheep were safely inside Mr. Lehman's truck (he was the cattle buyer). She had to round them up and let them go a couple of times. Our flock had given everyone concerned a run for their money—poor little lost sheep. Perhaps Elvida Johnson was the only one sorry to see her animals go—good old bossy-cow, who had given such wonderful milk and cream, but then a cow is also confining and she and Emory wanted to be free to go places together.

The school program commemorating Lincoln, Washington, and St. Valentine all-in-one was another little bright spot with Mrs. Shull and the children, singing and exchanging valentines while the mothers served hearts and tarts.

In March, I became a school board member for a four-year term; I was also teaching the girls their A-B-C's of music and piano playing. The first thing on the agenda was to advertise for a teacher for the 1958-59 school year, and board member Bob Burn wrote the following ad: "One-room school on Waldron needs teacher, preferably one with children. A cottage and fuel will be provided and the community offers an unhurried atmosphere, no electricity, phones, or ferry service; small mailboat three times a week, airplanes stop on call; there are no stores but there are a few cars and once there was a three-car collision." Clerk of the board, Lizanne Magraw, had added, "Beautiful setting, small school enrollment, no traffic, supervisors, or TV."

It was a hard decision to make as several good prospects responded to the ads. We chose the Reiss family as they had four school-age children. Mrs. Reiss (Annette) was a first grade teacher in Seattle and one of her past experiences was being the first person to teach in a Quonset hut school at Fort Richardson, Alaska, during the second World War.

Her husband, Tom, was a super salesman for a freezer concern. He and Annette and the children, Susan, Chuck, Mike, and Danny, arrived on the *Nordland* in June, saying it was the most eventful day in their lives and a dream come true. What we lacked in excitement, they were to provide.

They had a small cruiser, *Sputter-Nik*, they called it, and their first trip to Friday Harbor was one they wouldn't forget. They started off in good spirits until they passed the Oceanic Labs at the entrance to the harbor, where they hit the swirling currents. Then everything went awry. Danny fell overboard and Tom instantly let go of the wheel and was in after him. The boat swerved crazily, and Helen Ludwig, who was with them, tried to stop it by pushing and pulling all the gadgets until she pulled the choke. Cushions were thrown to Tom, who by then had Danny in tow, and Annette, who was feeling anything but calm, tried to reassure the children, who were all crying. Helen lost her shoes overboard in the shuffle while trying to steady the boat and hang onto Danny at the same time. During this little episode, "Commodore Gale" who was also heading for the Harbor, waved and called a greeting to them as he passed, oblivious to the tragedy which had just been averted.

There had been a great deal of merriment between the Democrats and the Republicans when the French's burro arrived on the mailboat. I heard that it made quite a speech on the deck and the kids loved it. Some of them had never seen a real live donkey before and they followed it as though it were the Pied Piper. *Dusty, the Democrat,* as we were to call it, soon became the boss of the barnyard—first it had a showdown with the ram; then Pixie, the milk goat, learned that it didn't pay to stick her head through the fence. Dusty had chewed off most of her whiskers.

With a parting toot from the *Denny M* which just about startled us out of our wits, Ed Martel made his last trip to the island in July, 1958, completing his four-year contract with the Post Office Department as mail carrier.

The mailboats and their crews certainly played an important role in our lives. These unsung heroes who came in fair weather or foul to effect the exchange of the incoming and outgoing mail. There was no letup in their steady schedule, leaving Anacortes at 6:30 a.m. and plying through the tortuous passes among the nine different islands on their route. The *Bristol* was next on the run and was owned and operated by Capt. Earl Butler. She was a sixty-foot vessel with a 135-horsepower diesel engine built in 1928 as a cannery tender for Bering Sea duty. The *Bristol* kept up a pace of 9½ knots and returned to Anacortes at 7:30 p.m. or later. It was a long day's work with nothing to break the monotony but the concern for fog, weather, and tides. The mail must go through!

Emory and Elvida Johnson, who were no strangers to the island, finally retired to their old homestead. Emory worked as a millwright and Elvida was a clerk in charge of Boeing's blueprint files, a very important and exacting position. Emory renovated their old living house and also kept a few chickens and sometimes turkeys. Elvida grew strawberries as big as hen's eggs and her flower garden was a joy to all passers-by.

The Chevalier place on the sandflats was also coming to life again. Bill senior was now a mate for the Washington State Ferries and he and Lizzie divided their time between Friday Harbor and Waldron, coming in the *Camanah*. Their daughter Marge was active in the business world and married to Dick Guard. They had one son, Ricky. Betty was now a registered nurse and married to Charles Nash; they had two boys, Nicky and Kelly. Lizzie was very happy with the expansion of her family.

Little Billy was not exactly little any more but a fine strapping young man and a confirmed fisherman. After his four years in the Navy he fished at the reef nets on Stuart Island and then owned his own troller, the *Service*. He was also handy with carpenter tools and had fixed up the old place. Their's was the oldest frame house on the island and was then nearly a hundred years old.

Franny too had matured and she and Billy, with their old quarrel forgotten, were dating again. A new relationship was developing between them that would lead to a happy and fruitful married life together.

The island had been teeming with summer folk and my sister, Madge, and her husband, Harold, were visiting. Jim had flown in with a shipmate, Mr. Rockhill, so up went the smoke signals and out went the carrier pigeons and everyone gathered for one of our famous dances.

Considered by some to be the best fish story of the week was the tale of what happened when Madge, Rocky, and I went out jigging in the row boat. I felt a hard pull on my line and said excitedly, "I think I have something." Rocky, who had a line out in the opposite side of the boat said, "I think I have something too." After seesawing back and forth for a few minutes we realized that all we had on our lines was each other—"out of the mouths of babes." It was young Danny Reiss who said, "The best way to communicate with a fish is to drop it a line."

The day was clear and cold but very pleasant as we gathered for our Waldron family Thanksgiving celebration. The leaves had fluttered away early that year but there were a few left to blend with the bronze chrysanthemums that brightened our tables. The dinner was the same fine meal with a golden brown turkey and all the trimmings, but the dance which followed later in the evening seemed to have advanced a century. In place of the old hand-wound phonograph, candles, and lamplight, we had a hi-fi system and electric light. The songs were strange and new. The babies who used to sleep peacefully under the tables and in the corners were up and at 'em with their new version of rock and roll. There was no *Little Swiss Waltz* for Squire Gale, no *String of Pearls* for Mark, no *Hernando's Hide-Away*, *Sparkling Wine*, *Blue Tango*, and the rest, all favorites of earlier times. With the coming of the Reisses the tempo of the island seemed to change. The quiet, unhurried atmosphere we had promised them turned hectic. One day, Annette came to the house to see me, leaving her Buick on the hill and forgetting to set the brakes. It took off for a slow-motion dive down the steep hill, mowing down a tree, taking out part of the fence, and landing into the rear of the post office building, conveniently missing the doorway. Fortunately, she had not insisted that the children stay in the car as she frequently did. The hood was ripped off with a resounding crash and the children were very frightened.

The following week there was a fire at the school cottage and Annette had gone right into action getting a good soaking trying to throw water up into the flames. She left the junior fire brigade to take over while she went for adult help. Mike and Susan dipped buckets of water from the rain barrel and passed them in relays to Denny on the ladder as he bravely emptied them into the flames. The damage was slight, but fire is always frightening and nothing looks so desolate as the scene afterwards with smoke, soot, charred wood, dripping water, shattered nerves, and dirty faces. This called for a school board meeting to discuss the repairs of the cottage, fire extinguishers, future fire drills, and insurance. It was *An ember to remember*, the Smokey Bear slogan that won first prize for Susanne Reiss.

In January of the new year it was back to the salt mines for my mate, and when he joined his ship in Seattle I went along for the ride to see how the other half of the family lived. I gingerly climbed the long gangways, dodged the swinging clam shells, as they called their loading apparatus, crossed the decks, and stumbled up the steep companionways to the officers' quarters. I tried to sleep in the bunk while all night long the grinding winches off-loaded the cargo of salt. Conditions may have improved from a century ago but a seaman's life is still a hard one. It is not a woman's world unless she is one of many pinned to the bulkheads, draped or undraped, upon the calendars.

Back on the island we had plum blossoms in February and Alice McDonald's peach tree was in bloom. I guess anything can happen in the San Juans—daffodils and wallflowers all about and folks planting peas while dodging snow flakes. Norman McDonald's third book, *Witch Doctor*, was soon to be on the market. There is never a dull moment in that rollicking good yarn of the old Indian tribes in Alaska, their customs and their first meeting with the white men, the *Hairy Faces*. It was new, different, and delightfully humorous.

With the arrival of Easter came new hope and happiness and a fresh start together for Fran and Billy. They were married at a quiet ceremony at the home of Ed and Avon McGinnis, son and daughter-in-law of Louise Gale and sister to Lizzie. The wedding was attended by the immediate family and a reception was given for them in Friday Harbor. Afterwards they left for their honeymoon at the Grand Coulee Dam.

Chapter Fourteen
The Waldron Word
1958-1960

Mr. Virgil Frits, editor of the *Friday Harbor Journal* for 51 years, retired in 1958. He came to Friday Harbor in 1906, working for the *Journal* and later in 1907 he became its owner and publisher. Mr. Frits was a great guy with a great cigar and ran a lively little paper; he considered his correspondents as members of the paper's family. It was great fun writing for him. Folks used to drop by his office just to say hello and their names would be put in the "Friday Harbor in a Nutshell" column as a *Journal* visitor.

I had stopped by to greet the new editor and publisher, Bob and Mildred Hartzog, from Oregon and seemingly things had not changed much around the office; the aroma was still the same and Virgil was sitting at this old desk smoking one of his famous cigars. After a jolly chat I left with a big wad of scratch paper under my arm and such an inflated ego I could hardly walk through the door. I was to spend many years as the official Waldron correspondent to the *Journal* and this chapter is largely excerpted from my column, "The Waldron Word."

Soon after the Hartzogs had taken over, they sent a form letter to all correspondents concerning the principles and methods of operation, the significance of advertising, space and news, and the importance that Mrs. Brown's going to town might have for a subscriber in the British West Indies. In other words, keep your columns brief. We couldn't always say why Mrs. Brown went to town, but when Squire Gale went to Friday Harbor for two consecutive weeks all dressed up in his Sunday best, it bore looking into, as did some old deeds. The aforesaid Squire was one of Waldron's landed gentry of long standing so it was quite a jolt to him to discover that the deed to his property was not in order, hence his visits to see Mr. Geneste, the lawyer. Many real estate deals that were signed by the local Justice of the Peace in the old days were proving to be legally unacceptable.

Reporting was rather a precarious business. You had to be all ears, go in where angels fear to tread, and be tactfully nosey. You can starve to death literally or be sued for libel.

* * *

I asked Mr. McDonald, the author, what was the purpose of his trip to Bellingham and he said he was going to see about a reservation at the poorhouse. Mac was such a joker and real happy too, recklessly squirting water all over the place. After digging three wells without any luck he struck an unlimited supply from the old Doucette well which for years had only given three buckets a day, one for the cow and two for Wealthy Mae.

When Mac removed some of the boards in the kitchen to do some plumbing he unearthed some ancient scrolls, the round childish handwriting of Margaret Severson, nee Kertula, and Louise Gale, nee Graignic, and some of the members of the old families. The boards were lined with copies of the Islander dated 1898 and 1902. They contained the same little news items of people coming and going to Whatcom, now known as Bellingham. The old ads were amusing: Sears and Roebuck sewing machines, high grade, polished antique oak finish, only $8.95; splendid waists of fine Mercer Satine, tucked, each only $1.25; some guy claiming he could cure fits, just send for his free bottle; and of course Lydia E. Pinkham's pink pills for pale people; porcelain crowns were the latest thing in dentistry, a boon to singers, increasing the acoustic effects of the voice.

Mr. McDonald's father wrote the items for Olga and when it was said of him that he was very versatile, he went around for days repeating the word; he wasn't quite sure of what it meant.

So the oldest log cabin on the island still standing now had running water, but Mac thought dipping it out of a barrel was quicker than waiting for it to run out of the faucet.

* * *

Through the medium of the post office department we were reminded of all kinds of National Weeks for this and that; there was even an annual

Mailbox Improvement Week. Waldron had a mailbox all right; it was required by postal regulations but no one ever used it. Inside it was a bird's nest and a little fledgling had peeked out at me with its beak wide open in anticipation of food. Now who could improve on anything like that?

At first I thought it was one of Emory Johnson's little jokes when he asked me if he could send ammunition through the mails, that he had a few cannon balls he wanted to send to Seattle. It was no joke and really presented quite a problem. One ball alone weighed 48 pounds. Wouldn't do to toss these onto the mailboat; I understand that was the original purpose of them, just to smash things all to pieces.

* * *

In a recent article on Waldron history, Jack Allen was pictured displaying these old cannon balls and two dead-eyes. The dead-eyes were from the rigging of the old converted sailing vessels that were used to transport sandstone blocks from the quarry at Pt. Disney, and the balls were ballast and probably used in the Pig War of the San Juans in 1860.

* * *

The following is what I called my sloop scoop. A man had fallen asleep, exhausted, and it was as though an unseen hand had piloted his $12,000 dollar, thirty-foot sailing sloop through the raging storm into a little wedge of beach between two menacing rocks on the north shore of Waldron. It was a hungry and bewildered gentleman who knocked on Margaret Severson's door one morning enquiring if her men folk were around, saying simply, "I am in trouble." Margaret was a little more than troubled herself, having problems with her washing machine, and wasn't expecting a shipwrecked mariner to call.

Over a life-renewing cup of coffee in Margaret's warm kitchen, Mr. Hunter told his story of how he was returning to his home in Vancouver, B.C., after visiting Saltspring Island, Victoria, and the States. Leaving Port Townsend the previous morning he ran into the storm, using up all his gas bucking it until he fell asleep and was blown into his present predicament—that was really a miracle.

Mr. Hunter thought he was on a deserted island as he climbed up over the rocks, passing Fishery Point and all the closed up cabins on the Sand Flats. Perhaps he thought he was in the Garden of Eden when he spied a tree bearing apples, in January yet. He bit into one hungrily and put a few in his pocket. He had nothing to eat on the sloop. (How improvident these gentlemen sailors are sometimes!)

He then retraced his steps and his spirits rose as he saw some young stock in a meadow and came upon fresh tractor tracks which led him to Margaret's door and a hearty breakfast. Margaret, knowing full well the whims of the sea and tides, had enough presence of mind to know that a message must be sent off by the mailboat and remembered that Norman McDonald would be by shortly to pick up her mail. So Mac took the message and Mr. Butler of the *Bristol* relayed it to the Coast Guard, who came directly, releasing the sloop from her berth and towing it to Friday Harbor shipyard.

* * *

There was a happy hubbub and welcome cries when the mailboat brought the Weavers back for the summer. Nipper, their dog, who was a native son, went wild when he heard the cry of a seagull. Mary and Bob and the family, Josie, Nellie, Chris, and Andy, had driven across country from Goshen, Indiana, to the promised land and made their home in Mount Vernon. This was a step nearer to their final goal of setting on Waldron.

* * *

Jim and I were soon to celebrate our new status as grandparents when Fran and Billy had their first child, Cindy. I was living in an exclusive world set apart for grandmothers, such goo-ings and goings on. It was sort of a family reunion with Jim home on vacation, Phil coming from New York, their sister, Stella, and her husband, Dr. Norman Fiske, all together for the first time and enjoying the simple everyday events with much enthusiasm—digging and tasting steamer clams, fishing for cod from the rocks in view of Mt. Baker, gathering evergreen blackberries, or just sitting and watching the ever-changing sky and water at sunset.

* * *

Like all good things, our fleeting summer came to an end and the cricket's plaintive little song would remind us that autumn was at hand with misty, moisty mornings, changing colors, and ripening fruit. In the early morning I would hear hundreds of little birds in the Madrona tree just outside my window, having their breakfast of orange-red berries.

According to Fred McNaught, it was a sign of a mild winter when the birds were not in a hurry to go south, staying to eat the berries. And to think that the lowly little woolly-bear caterpillars play a part in shaping our winters. From the same source I learned that if they had a wide brown band in the middle and a small black spot on each end it also was a sign of a mild winter. Fred had found one that fit this description.

* * *

In the fall, the school board was faced with the problem of finding a teacher and another interesting little family came in response to our teacher ad. The Tiptons, Robert and Elvern and their three little girls, Judith, Connie, and Cynthia, traveled all the way from the state of Maine. They fit well into the scheme of things.

Bob Tipton was experienced in carpentry and stone masonry and this was my chance to realize a long-hoped-for dream of having a fireplace. Over the years I had collected some fine specimens of rock from all the beaches around the island and loving neighbors brought their offerings of cherished pieces for the cause. Bob had been very patient while I hand-picked my chrysolite and porphyry, granite and schist for the finished product inside. It was one of my many blessings and when it was finished called for a celebration and christening at Thanksgiving that all the home folks attended.

The new year was the beginning of course-changing for Jim when his company, Olympic Steam, discontinued the salt run. His next assignment was to sail deep water carrying gifts of handshake grain to Indochina, a three and a-half month voyage. After celebrating Christmas with our new little family we said our farewells and Godspeed.

There was a change in the mailboat operation when Mr. Butler, because of ill health, had to give up his contract. My son-in-law, Billy, had been a member of the crew of the *Bristol* for about three months and he knew the routine and postal procedures and being an ambitious and dependable young man he took the responsibility of buying the *Bristol* and took over the mail contract. His father, Bill Sr., skippered the vessel for awhile. They continued to carry passengers and freight and were available for Saturday and Sunday charters.

Some too hasty spring-like weather had a little setback when the northeast wind returned to blow, preparing the way for snow which covered the crocuses and leafed-out shrubs with a deep white blanket. Some of us may sigh, and justly so, because of the inconvenience of driving to work with messy road conditions. Some would rather see it from inside where it is cozy and warm. But if you had an opportunity to walk out in it and observe all its aspects, it would lift your spirits and put roses in your cheeks, watching the gradual transformation of the countryside with its soft white beauty, perhaps helping to guide some bewildered sheep and their lambs to shelter and food, or watching the fat robins scrounging for tidbits. When the sun shines, making picturesque shadows and sparkling lights, I would get carried away.

Three and a half months was a long time to be without my mate and I would find myself into some predicaments when it came to machinery. Mr. McDonald used to call me Diz and Calamity Jane. One morning I had trouble starting the washing machine and I made up a mixture from different cans in the oil house, marked Standard Oil, liquid floor wax, RPM-SAE-30, and Valvoline, and had put it into the engine. I absentmindedly dumped a half package of Tide, king-sized, into the wash and I was almost overcome with the fumes and soap suds. I was reluctant to seek advice from a neighbor since my last episode when I broke up a supper party to tow my truck out of a mud hole. The soap suds reminded me of the time Jim tried to cook a whole package of macaroni on the galley stove; macaroni was all over the place. So I learned a little knowledge is a dangerous thing and when mixing motor oil, smell before using.

There was never an idle moment, and the spring would bring people back to the island. Lou Gale, who would spend her winters with her grandchildren, would roll in on the mailboat to tend to her house and garden while listening to the familiar croaking of the frogs.

Living on a remote island can be real fun, especially for the children. All kinds of important people come to see them: Santa and his Christmas ship crew, Captain Puget of TV, Tiny Lloyd, Barney "Keep Washington Green" Furseth, and Bob "Smokey Bear" Moore. Writers visit to do feature articles about them and they even appeared on a television show.

Since TV had never monopolized our lives, it could still be a novelty; it was a real adventure for our sixteen youngsters to gather around the set of Elvida and Emory Johnson's one evening to watch the *Captain Puget Show* with the deep sea diver, the fish shenanigans, and Scottish dancers. It was a thrill to see themselves on the screen. It was befitting that the Waldron part had been shot in the home of two real sea captains, Captain Lovering and Captain Wood, who went to sea in the old sailing ships. I am sure my father would be happy to know that Captain Puget was helping to keep alive the old sea chanties which had been his favorite songs.

What is so different about Waldron? Some say it is the air, and Doe Burn would take deep sniffs of it, saying there is no place like it. Ah! Sweet spring with its fragrant little lady slippers and flowering currant. Connie Tipton called it Dollar Day when she and her sisters picked up twelve sand dollars on the beach.

Easter vacation was always a memorable time when most of our old friends and clans would gather for communion and reunion. There were over 50 who met for the Easter brunch in and around the Tiberghien's home on the sand flats. The Tipton family was the only one to tackle the early morning hike to see the shrouded sunrise from Point Disney. After the morning mists had rolled away the day was sparkling fresh, leaving nothing to be desired except that Jim could be there.

We met in Portland in the middle of May when Jim successfully completed his voyage of sailing half way around the world. It was quite a story to relate but the seamen say it is all in a day's work; the gales and mountainous seas, the threat of fuel shortage, refrigeration failure, more storms and a lost anchor, extreme heat, and a few hours in a foreign port to see the sights and buy a few trinkets for the folks back home. Monotony and homesickness and the eternal sea, it gets in their blood, and after ten days in home port they are ready to do it all over again. They were to make a return trip to Calcutta, India, carrying another cargo of wheat.

Birthday celebrations for the children were as much a part of island living as growing up itself. The cake creations were usually works of art and for the children, the beach and the woods were their Sears Roebuck, and mother's sewing bag their Frederick and Nelson's. They were equally as creative with their gifts from the sea, miniature carvings and intricate patterned shells made into pins; and pieces of their own hand-weaving, pot holders, and the like.

Lizanne Magraw was the master cake builder and for Linnea it was a pale blue chiffon dotted with iridescent pearly-tops and six candles, the peak of perfection which caused sighs of pleasure. The cake for her sister, Allison, brought gasps of delight. It was an old English garden with rich dark chocolate earth covered with green coconut grass and a prim white picket fence with miniature rose bushes (double red hawthorne). It was a masterpiece of culinary art.

No wonder I had stayed awake half the night dreaming up something comparable to serve at my piano recital several days later. I came up with a pale yellow slab covered with multi-colored musical notes, bass and treble clefs, and rests. Teaching the children the A-B-C's of music was more up my alley and it was fun. On the last day of school, folks came down to the dock to see the Tiptons off. After a year of teaching and pleasant associations, we found it hard to say goodbye to this good little family.

Members of the school board met under the cherry trees at Alice McDonald's to draw up a contract for Lizanne Magraw, who was to be the next teacher. I had been elected to serve in her place as clerk of the board. We also reviewed the unusual conditions arising from the unprecedented increase in enrollment which included three junior high students who would be taking correspondence courses. The desirability of staying on Waldron had appealed to several families and individuals so the once estimated attendance of five pupils had grown to a possible sixteen, which meant practically all grades in a one-room school.

It was considered a privilege to attend school on the island; what it may lack in competition and sports they seem to make up in a broadness of rare experience.

For ten years Irving French had been investigating all modes of communication to find a simple system whereby we could make emergency calls, but, up until then, his efforts had been fruitless and thwarted with complications, international agreements, regulations, mobile and immobile technicalities, prohibitive costs, and the fact that he was not living in the right location. But at last he had hit upon a simple method of communication to the outer world with no strings attached. Irving was the first to make and receive a test call from his Viking Messenger C.B. set which he had installed in his truck. Others were soon to buy sets, including Jim and me, and were usually asked what were their megacycles.

It seemed so right to have one of Ethan Allen's grandchildren come back to Waldron to make her home here on the old homestead. Marjorie North and her husband, Wayne (Corky), and their two children, Larry and Chet, officially moved here from Orcas Island and started to build a new house on the highly coveted little point which had been my favorite fishing spot on the north shore of Mail Bay. Corky had hopes of putting in floats and a marine service station for use during the summer months. They called it Juniper Cove Ranch.

Birds! Birds! Birds! We were all mad at the birds. Woe was ours. Between pigeons and crows our entire crop would be gone. All efforts to scare or ward them off seemed futile. Hanging a dead brother crow nearby, or silvery jingles, shrouding a favorite tree in a mantle of cheesecloth, and keeping constant vigil were all of no avail. They would carry the cherries off right under our noses. It was a real problem all right, but considering the woes of the world in general, not a very big one.

I always felt that I got my money's worth when flying to Seattle with Island Sky Ferries. On a clear day it's a bird's eye view of the mountains and waterways, seeing things in miniature, like toy ships, trains, doll houses, farms, docks and buildings, and a colorful mosaic of parked cars. I was on my way to meet Captain Jim who was back from another Indian sea voyage. He was on vacation and together we made a leisurely trip of the Olympic Peninsula. I wanted to stay another night but Jim said, "No!" and kept saying, "I want to see the kids," meaning Fran, Bill, and Cindy, as though he had a presentiment of something to happen. Occasionally, Fran would accompany Bill on the *Bristol* staying overnight in Anacortes and on this particular night when she started to have pains Fran thought she had eaten too many cherries. Fortunately, doctor and hospital were close at hand and we arrived just in the nick of time as our grandson, Matthew James Chevalier, was born in the wee small hours on July 25, 1960, surprising everyone with his early arrival. For the next few days our courses were laid out for us. Jim ran the *Bristol* while I took care of Cindy.

Meanwhile, on the island, we saw the geese flying southward, our beautiful red and gold leaves fast becoming exhausted, sodden, and subdued by the rain after their whimsical frolic with the wind. Apples, squash, and pumpkins were harvested and the remnants of the garden tucked away as the glorious month of October came to a close.

Everyone was in a flurry of mysterious excitement as they took flights of fancy to the far corners of the globe, while scrounging in the trunks and rag bags hunting for jewelry and bright scarves, as they secretly imagined themselves playing an exotic role in the land of make believe. An eerie misty moon shone over the creaky old schoolhouse at the crossroads while the owls in the dark woods nearby screeched at the motley company of ghosts, medieval figures, and gypsies; storybook characters were all coming to partake of the witches' potluck brew and to join in the pranks and games of Halloween. The musical chairs were truly unruly and everyone was wise to Red Riding Hood, the Caliph, and Friar Tuck as they cavorted with the Spanish dancer who good humorously gave way to the elves and pixies while a little two-faced clown stole the show. In spite of Marc Antony's efforts to revitalize the old phonograph, it had just wailed out some ghostly tunes and then died away. An accommodating witch then conjured up some of her craft on the piano and there was spirited dancing until Halloween gave up the ghost.

The same spirit of camaraderie prevailed at Thanksgiving when folks gathered around the festive tables to give thanks for a good harvest and all the blessings of home and family. Forty-six was the official count at our island family dinner and it was feared for awhile we would have some uninvited guests as some turkey gobblers insisted on following the crowd to the post office. Roy Bucknell, after several attempts, got them penned up and he had to run for his life as the hens all flew over the fence after him. After this little flurry of excitement we settled down to the business of hearty eating.

Soon we were to find ourselves in the middle of the mail-order muddle, the children's hope and mothers' fears. Our post office is a rather important place as the Christmas rush is upon us but if the mailboat is a little later than usual with its extra heavy load, folks can sit back and enjoy a cup of coffee which I kept hot on the big blackbellied stove or fireplace.

Jingle, Jingle, Jingle, here comes Kris Kringle. Neither the early hour nor the wind nor rain would keep families from coming to the dock to meet this rotund and ageless old man from the far north. Then Waldron's own special treat to enjoy was the program at the schoolhouse, an original play entitled *The Gifts of the Cuckoo*. It was directed by Lizanne Magraw and enacted by the school children with delightful charm and natural poise. Andy Weaver, the youthful writer, showed an extraordinary insight into the essence of Christmas giving, as his play demonstrated this rare truth about good will to men, that the simple gifts of love are more to be desired than gold.

My family—I am the blonde haired little girl at my father's side.

Jim and Ralph Wood grading for the store site, August, 1936.

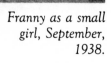

Franny as a small girl, September, 1938.

Photo taken at Jack and Ruth Allen's fiftieth wedding anniversary. First standing row, left to right: Irving French, Bill Chevalier, Sr., Lizzy Chevalier, Goodie Goodrich, Ralph Wood, Jack Magraw, Mildred Ludwig, me, Louise Gale, Marjorie French, Millie Thorson with her son Rolf, Margaret Severson, and the "bride" Ruth Allen. Second standing row, left to right: Elvida Johnson, Emory Johnson, Doe Bum, Josie Weaver, Bob Bum peering around with his son Mark, John Goodrich, Mark Hayes, Dorothy Bucknell, Mary Tiberghien, Captain Wood, Mary Weaver, Ray Tiberghien, Stanley Gale, Jack Allen. Last row, tall man is Chuck Ludwig, small boy is Nils Thorson. Children in the front first row, left to right: Susan Bucknell, Paul Goodrich, Chris Weaver, Cameron Bum (standing), Steve Ludwig. Second row, left to right: Rick Guard, Andy Weaver, Joe Goodrich. Third row, left to right: Donny Bucknell, Jimmy Bucknell, one of the Bum girls, Peer Thorson. The Magraw girls are grouped together behind them and little Mary Ludwig stands to the right.

Jim and I in front of our first home on Waldron with the new porch addition and a few flowers.

Interior of the Waldronia Store, August, 1937.

Hardworking Bob Jones with a batch of fresh eggs, October, 1939.

*Jim and I working
in the woods.*

*A meadow and
Cowlitz Bay in the
spring — just one of the
lovely scenes around
the bend from the
dock.*

The Bristol *at
Waldron Dock.*

June and Farrar Burn in front of their cozy cabin.

Our one-room school house in 1951 when we had only two pupils.

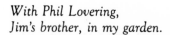

With Phil Lovering, Jim's brother, in my garden.

Mae Doucette, one of the island's wonderful, hearty characters. She was once a dancehall girl.

A view up North Bay.

Chapter Fifteen
"10-4, This Is Waldron"
1961-1962

Early in January a new milestone in the island's history was reached. It was through the continued efforts of Irving French and Dave Richardson of Orcas that antennas were erected and two more Viking Messengers put into operation and added to the network of radio transceivers connecting the islands. These sets brought the first direct communication between Waldron and Friday Harbor. It took a little getting used to, to manipulate the perfect squelch, not to put the transmitter to your ear and only talk when Roger says over.

After that our radio system continued to grow with much testing and trying out new locations to find the best possible reception and service from the available transceivers. One site was being tried at Double Island, and Buzz Sheehan, the grocer on Orcas, had joined the network; and a new location was being tested in Friday Harbor.

Waldron had its first emergency when Margaret Wood became suddenly ill; a call from our set to Mr. Smith at Deer Harbor brought Dr. Heath within the hour. Waldron added to Dr. Heath's long list of emergencies when John Heider, one of the Gale's grandsons, tangled with a chain saw which had ripped up his arm quite badly. It took three hours and 99 stitches to repair him.

People always wondered how we had managed without direct communication. Although it was rather primitive we did have a system that worked pretty well. When there was sickness or an emergency, a letter was sent by the mailboat or the signal flag was raised and, pronto, a plane from Island Sky Ferries would circle and medicine would be dropped at our doorstep. We never lost a bundle.

One day it was necessary to summon Dr. Heath for Fred McNaught, who had a severe case of shingles. Helen Ludwig and I had difficulty flagging down the plane. The northeast wind hampered our attempts to hold the flagpole in place, so with the tools at hand, an old bent spading fork and a coal scoop, we dug its hole deeper, putting in some rocks and tamping down the earth like a couple of professional post hole diggers. An old sheet and a few safety pins did the rest of the trick and the ever-alert Flyboys brought the doctor over promptly.

"WHALE SIGHTED IN DIPSEE BAY!" Thar she blew and not a harpoon in the crowd; the magnificent killer whales are indeed a part of Waldron. Ralph Wood kept his distance and Bob Weaver wasn't interested in whaling, he was angling for ling and he had caught a whopper. Its white flesh is quite superior when it goes into the fry pan directly from the sea.

When we first discovered abalone hereabouts we thought that rumors of the water turning warmer in the San Juans might be true and that the abalones were moving up here from California. After a little research, I learned that they were an obscure species, *Haliotus Kamtschatkana*, resident to certain areas of the northern coastline. They are really a marine gastropod (a polite name for snail) having a shell lined with mother-of-pearl. They have to be pried from the rocks and only the foot is eaten and some special know-how is needed to remove them from their shell. The discoverers had a great time preparing them after consulting an old cookbook. The trick is to pound the muscle until it relaxes and then it is ready for the frying pan, with some butter. It is delicious.

Our pigeons were right back on time in the spring working on the greening cherries and seedlings. It is indeed a complex world, but the flowers are a beautiful and deceptively simple looking creation of nature.

There was a lovely spring vegetable garden with cabbages in neat rows which were all eaten up on Doe Burn's birthday. We enjoyed another cake creation by Lizanne, and part of a surprise party given for her. When the birthday song rang out with candles alight, Doe reached for my fireplace bellows and extinguished the candles with four little puffs. She explained, since she had a slight cold it was more sanitary that way. Our little musical group chose this occasion to give a practice concert in Doe's honor. Julia Segovia DeHart bravely set her music aside and charmed us all by playing, by heart, a selection of 17th century pieces on her concert guitar. Nimble fingers Mary Weaver, pianist, accompanied Tony Scruton as he played his magic flute. Frances, the Lark, as I like to call myself, sang a couple of songs and played piano duets with Mary. In conclusion there was a lilting trio of piano, flute, and voice performing *Auf Dem Wasser Zu Singen*, (To Be Sung on the Waters) composed by Schubert.

I had often been called the "far flung and foreign correspondent" whenever I was called away to the city to keep a rendezvous with my captain. With the exception of a few intensive storms on the way over, this trip to East Pakistan had been just routine for my old salt. We met in Seattle and celebrated our 28th wedding anniversary, then came home on the *Bristol* loaded with gear, groceries, and plants, eager to start on some new projects together. I had already hung up a slate in the galley headed *Jobs for Jim* to which someone had added, "work, work, work."

When the Olympic Steamship Company sold their last ship they went out of business. Jim had worked for them for fifteen years or more so he was left high and dry, so to speak, but not for long. He went aboard as relief Captain on the mailboat M.V. *Bristol* for three days a week while Bill Chevalier took it easy and went gillnetting with young Bill. Billy's operator's license was insufficient for the number of passengers they carried so this arrangement worked out well.

Down through the years, Lyle Place had been the appointed spot for the Fourth of July island picnic, with its phantom owner's permission to use and enjoy that stretch of sandy beach taken for granted. The sand flat was carpeted with sweet wild verbena and backed with evergreens and feathery spirea, and the view took in the distant misty mounds across the glistening waters and the splendor of the sun as it sank into the netherlands. The long picnic tables of yesteryear had long since crumbled away and faded with the legends of old settlers. Now the long silent stretches of waterfront are alive with new owners, cruisers, and summer homes springing up everywhere. A few fir trees up from the Scotts were the Minklers, and the Breckenridges were somewhere in between. A picnic is a picnic the world over; the messes of potage were many, the victuals were vast and varied. In other words there was lots to eat and lots of people to eat with and meet with. The nose count was 92.

When Marjorie French's twelfth grandchild was born she said she was beginning to believe that babies were only for young folk. I was just in my heyday and was a member of the Silly Old Picture Packing Grammas (SOPPG's). My granddaughter, Cindy, the "Terrible Tiny," ruled the roost. I had been dubbed Nana Nono and later Nana Nincompoop when I let Matthew fall out of his crib. I forgot to tie him in. It was all so wonderful. Cindy was learning her letters and numbers; they went something like this: 14W-2086, 14Q-0839, Over. Children do catch on quickly. I called her from another room and she answered, "I don't read you, Gramma, I don't read you."

Things were bubbling over at Mac's distillery and Alice's wine list was almost complete with blackberry, apple, rose hip and parsnip, dandelion and hawthorn. There was no end to the possibilities of her fascinating hobby. Mac says that one blackberry in the crock is worth two in the bushes. A little book that Alice brought from England told how to make delicious wine for less than a shilling a bottle. She had to call in an expert when it called for caster sugar; and where to find an ounce of 'ops and a sprig of mace?

* * *

Said Grandpa Lovering on one of his days off, "Let's go fishing." This is the way the story was told to the grandchildren, when Jim and I set out to sea one day.

"You may swear a little, Darling," said I.

"Oh, Honey, if I were a woman I would cry," said Jim.

He had all sorts of lures and gadgets and he was showing his latest one to Honey, who was a little dubious.

"It's for you, dear, to catch a ling cod. See, triple hook and stainless steel, can't corrode," said Jim.

"For me? Well, that's nice, but ling cod are so big, wouldn't know how to handle one. Just give me a little hook and a minnow to dangle. Rock cod is big enough for me. If I get snagged with one of those things, bingo, there goes a dollar-ten."

Honey thought she could be ready by four. The tide would be just right and it would be a perfect evening to angle and to watch the ever-changing tints reflected in the slack waters as they drifted along, to hear the soft cooing of the little sea birds gently rocking on the kelp beds in the quiet stillness.

"But, Darling, the girls are coming over for a meeting, we have to work out the school calendar," said I.

Honey had to think fast, how to bake her cookies and go pick up the girls. Lizanne had trouble again and had to leave her car on the road. The boys who were shaking the post office roof would need a lemonade break, gets awfully hot up there in the afternoon sun. He had everything ready, the outboard sitting up where it should be, the boat was on the trailer; it hadn't been in the water for a spell so a few parts needed freeing up. Gas, life jackets, tackle box, poles, seats and cushions, gaff hook, and—"Oh, Honey, do you know where the brass polish is, and those pearl wobblers? I think they are on your desk."

Honey hunts all over. "Darling, I can't find them, what did you do with the sack?"

"What sack?" No, these were some he bought a couple of months ago with an assortment of hooks and sinkers.

"Oh, Sweetheart, when is Easter?" said I.

"How should I know, let's get going."

"Don't you think we should have a thermos of coffee, gets kind of cool after the sun goes down," said I.

"Well, it might be a good idea, but hurry."

The girls suggest putting on some warm clothing, the night air and all. Honey considers; wool slacks, extra sweater, cap and gloves, a wool scarf. It reminds her of the time she caught her first salmon when the hooknose silvers invaded the bay, years ago.

"Well, goodbye and good luck," this from the girls, still trying to figure when Easter would be in the year 1962. Off they went to the beach, trailer unhitched and backed down into the water with a minimum of puffing as it bogged down in the gravel, but finally they glide out into smooth water. Honey, perspiring under her bundling, knew she would need it once the boat was in motion.

"Oh, Sweet, why don't you polish up those flashers?" said I.

"But I polished them the last time."

"I know, but you have to do it every time."

Br br brr brrr, a nice healthy sound issued from the motor as Honey settled down with a sigh.

"What's the matter?" Something was wrong, the boat wasn't moving. Darling said quietly, "We might as well go home, I can't get her into gear." At times she believes he is a descendant of Job.

"Say, Sweetheart, hand me the bight of that rope," said Jim. Honey brightens and decides he means the loop at the end.

"No, not that, the bight." Honey, confused, tries again and fails; then a little irked says, "If you wouldn't use those nautical terms and tell me that you mean the middle of the rope, maybe I could understand what you want."

"Oh, Darling, how did you say Easter was figured?" said Jim.

"The first Sunday after the first full moon after the vernal equinox. Anyone could tell you that."

"I need that cup of coffee," said Jim.

* * *

Oh, ye old Indian summer, what a day for our yearly cider bee. It took place at the same old spot at the Magraw's. There was the same abundance of juicy apples, good fun, and food, but alas! it couldn't be said that it was the same old grind. Ye olde, olde, cider press went modern when Emory Johnson rigged it up with a horse-and-a-half. Under the circumstances it was rather an advantage since most of our vigorous youth had deserted us and our community was dwindling. June and Farrar came to join in the fun. Where there was Farrar there was always furor. We were seeing more of him since Ralph Wood gave up his rural mail route. Still the friendly troubadour, Farrar had his moments and at one time he was laying down the law to some passers-by for shooting from their boat. They wanted to know, "Don't you want to get rid of your crows?" He told them in no uncertain terms that he would take care of his crows and them too if they came trespassing in his gulch, but, "Wait, aren't you Farrar Burn?" Well, "I am Doctor So-and-so, I knew you when..." "Well, I'll be durned, come on in and meet the wife." They were practically kissing one another.

The house looked as if a cyclone had struck. It had, as Cyclone Cindy had left books, balls, blocks, and "babas" in her path. I was just beginning to unwind after a stint in Friday Harbor with Fran and the latest member of the Chevalier family, Marty William. Coming from a family of ten, I still wonder how they managed in my mother's day.

Trouble seemed to come in bunches and November was calamity month. It was that last mighty heave in his endeavor to close the crack in the new water tank that dealt Jim a cruel blow—the wrench slipped and the pipe flew off, hitting him in the face. It caved in his cheek bone and cracked his jaw. He had to be taken to Bellingham to have it set and wired. Norman McDonald was sorely distressed, feeling that he may have cracked a rib while working on *his* water system. Then wham, bang, Bob Weaver was seeing stars when the peevee he was using slipped and hit him in the jaw.

We thought it was high time to bring out the big Halloween pot and stir up a brew to ward off the evil spirits. But it didn't work, the worst catastrophe was yet to come. On the night of November 22nd, the mailboat *Bristol* collided with a Canadian barge. It happened shortly after Billy and his deckmate Leslie (Dutch) Anderson were leaving Blakely on their way to Urban on Sinclair Island. In a matter of only four minutes the vessel went under. As the *Bristol* was sinking, the men struggled into the lifeboat which was secured on the top of the pilot house. When the water reached it the men tried to push the lifeboat out away from the boom that was lodged under one of the stays. When the lifeboat finally broke loose it was filled with water and floated to the surface, but the weight of the water and the men caused it to capsize. The men threw themselves thwartships across the lifeboat and hung on until the tug boat *Anna Gore* released its lines to the barge and came to the rescue. Twenty minutes later they were pulled from the water by the Coast Guard.

The *Bristol* was in 33 fathoms of water with ten sacks of first class mail and a dozen sacks of parcel post packages aboard; these were recovered later. We were shocked and distressed over the fate of the *Bristol* and the watery ordeal of its crew and the little dog, Susie, but thankful that they all had made it home safely. My Jim and Charles Nash then carried the mail on the cannery tender *Nereid* until Billy made arrangements to replace the ill-fated *Bristol*.

In a lighter vein, Irving French thought that all married couples should have a fallout shelter, and Norman was thinking seriously of moving into one when he and Alice had a near-fallout over an opera incident. Saturdays were set aside for transistor opera at the McDonald's and the season had opened with Joan Sutherland in *Lucia di Lammermoor*. Alice and Andy Weaver sat entranced during an aria from the mad scene while Mac and Tony Scruton were absorbed in a game of chess. La Stupenda was reaching her full, rich, high E-flat and the chess players chose this sublime moment to exclaim loudly over a move. It was downright sacrilege and tempers flared. Albeit, Alice later declared that all was forgiven.

We were so downhearted with so many disasters, accidents, and sickness so close to home that we had a hard time counting our blessings. Nevertheless, we didn't have to look far. The New Year's Eve celebration had not exactly been like old times but there was one lively spot with music and dancing and sipping and sampling of various verdant vintages at Tonio's Bistro. It was a picnic right up to the end when they all piled into the planes New Year's Day, with packsacks, bed rolls, and suitcases. They had waited at the field since early morning. Bellingham was fogged in so a bonfire was kept burning while Mary Weaver staved off growing appetites. Just about dusk, Island Skyboys arrived to take them to Mt. Vernon, the only spot on the coast that was open.

At times it had been so foggy flyers wouldn't know whether to take their waterwings or harps—now they were up and now down, skirting the mainland, then flying above the fog bank, so eerie below and beautiful above, like gliding on a huge meringue in sight of Mt. Baker, glistening with snow in the sunshine and blue sky. Just like life. If we could only remove the pall in between so our destination could be seen more clearly!

January was a wild one. The wintry blasts swooped down out of the northeast surrounding us with a fiercely cold kind of beauty, with the sun shining on the deep rolling sea, setting pink and mauve on the mountain ranges. Then the moonlight—wow! It came as a challenge and exhilaration to some but worked a hardship on others, especially Jim and Billy who were now running the mailboat *Aloma* and making every effort humanly possible to pick up and deliver the mail throughout the islands. Fran was here with the children and she loved to bundle them up, face into the wind, and bring in the wood. It reminded her of her childhood on the island, recalling the morning the kitchen door blew open during the night and there were drifts of snow in the house. It was five degrees above *inside*. We had no radios then to check the whereabouts of the mailboat; we just had to watch, wait, and wonder.

Miss Elsie Scott, county nurse and a faithful friend in sickness and health, made her last visit to the island before her retirement. After a booster breakfast of sour-dough hot cakes (a Weaver specialty) she gave booster shots to the school children. We remember her fondly for her devoted service to mankind.

Bob Weaver's dream baby, Tri-X-313, the seedless watermelon which he and his family, in collaboration with his brother-in-law, Dr. Eigsti, in Indiana, had worked and studied to perfect, was now available from the Burpee Seed Co. It is a small, deliciously sweet, family-sized melon.

As Tony Scruton eagerly alighted from the plane his first words were, "Has anything exciting been happening on the island?" We offered, "Well, the Frenches have a new tandem bicycle, Mrs. Lovering has a neck stretcher and 'hangs' herself every day, Marty Chevalier lodged his pacifier thwartships in his mouth and almost choked." Then it was spring with hosts of golden daffodils. That should be excitement enough for anyone.

There was great excitement and hardly enough room in the skiff for all the halibut the Guards and the Chevs hauled in, enough fish for the whole island. The location and bearings of this secret halibut hole were only known by a few of the old timers. I remember when Ethan Allen's son, Harvey, caught one that weighed a hundred pounds. I thought that being such a large fish it might be tough, but Harvey gave us a slice from the center and it was as tender as a young chicken.

If you have pumped water by hand or drawn it from a well for years there is a thrill drawing it from a faucet for the first time. Billy had put in the necessary pipe, tank, and pump engine for his folks. Lizzie said she never thought she would live to see the day. When one gets older a few of these things which others take for granted can be a blessing.

June Burn had been doing nothing for days and days but standing in the doorway watching and listening for a plane which might bring her son, North, onto the island. He came for a couple of weeks, renewing old acquaintances, catching up with all the changes on the island, visiting Sentinel Island where he was born, and seeing his brother, Bob, who came for the weekend. North had resigned from the Foreign Diplomatic Service after eleven years to accept a post as Assistant to the President of Mills College in Oakland, California, something he had wished to do for many years. His friendly charm, confidence and ability to put you at ease would banish from the mind that he was crippled with polio, and his spirits were high as he manipulated the rocky places and beachwood ramps which Farrar had prepared for him. His wife, Babs, and their two children were still in Paris.

Learning that North was an interested adult beginner at piano, the music practice group had invited him to their Tuesday session. After all the diplomatic *must* affairs, he was really impressed with the genuine friendliness and closeness of the people here. He had visited in Friday Harbor, seeing the Chevaliers, Lizz and Bill, Marge, Betty, and Billy, who were his boyhood playmates, and "Ma" who had brought him into the world on Sentinel Island during a wild northeaster while "Pa" went after Dr. Capron. It was so refreshing in that time of indecision and criticism of the high places to find a man so thoroughly human and with such faith in his country.

First prize sloganists, honor roll students, tennis and chess champions were among some who had attended our little one-room school, and then came the news that Anore Bucknell was the second young woman to reach the top of Alaska's 20,000-foot Mt. McKinley. Of course, she hadn't done it alone, there being five men with her, an ideal situation for any young lady. Nevertheless, Anore had always set her sights high and usually attained her objectives.

Everything turned out just right for the school picnic; the wind went down and the sun came up and the whole island gathered at the old Frank Graignic place where a gentle zephyr rippled over the rolling grasses, which then had covered what used to be acres of strawberries. In Frank's time these berries were famous for being first on the market. Content sitting on a convenient log or walking barefoot in the sand, we enjoyed our potluck to the fullest. Pomp and ceremony had been dispensed with and Chris Weaver was presented with an eighth grade diploma accompanied by a few well-chosen words while the class modestly displayed their school sewing jobs which they were wearing. The birds overhead did most of the singing but snatches of song and witty ditties could be heard from time to time from our old master warbler, Ray Tiberghien.

"Heigh Ho! Come to the fair!" Ho Hum! They came to the Seattle World's Fair and they came to the island. They brought their sleeping bags and enjoyed our clean air. We put on our best show, we gave them stars for a blanket and a silvery moon for a light. The murmuring sea lapped out a lullaby while the graceful gulls stood their night watch.

They came from Indiana to see the Weavers; we gave them a cool breeze and a green scene to rest their eyes. From California came sister Geva and Mabel and her family; we gave them oysters on the half shell, a low-low tide to dig clams, a string of herring hooks to experience the thrill of dodging the dogfish to bring in a shiny mess of fish and to enjoy their delicate flavor.

From the Fair city itself came the Gordons; Flash, and their growing family. Mike, their oldest son, favored the press with a preview of his piano composition which he called *Dry Ice*; it was real cool and he was very talented. Everyone asked that summer, "What has become of our salmon?" I couldn't answer that one but we all knew where the birds were. They had all come to Waldron. Alice McDonald said after last year's cheesecloth tents and billets under the trees she conceded the battle to the birds, with her blessing. We are angry at the crows who have denuded our cherry trees and the robins who absconded with our raspberries, but what would we do without the little birds that charm us at our windows and sing to us at eve? Poets and lyricists are inspired by them and cameras click to capture them swaying on the tall grasses or lined up on a wire.

Sharks, whales, sea lions—now came a new underwater menace, the wet suit shoot. Tony Scruton came up with a sea cucumber, *Cucumbaria frondosal*. They are repulsive looking things and it is a rather unpleasant task to prepare them. The slimy, slippery skin must be peeled back to secure the tender white muscle that is quite a delicacy when sauteed in butter.

We were now calling Jim the dogfish king. After the *Aloma* was taken off the mail run our old friends, Earl and Edith Butler, brought the mail in the *Moby Dick*. In the interim, Jim ran the *Aloma* for George Jeffers and Co., owners of the Friday Harbor Cannery, in connection with an experimental operation which could have been a boon to fishermen. Everyone had been talking about the dogfish which infested our waters; now someone was trying to do something about them. People have been known to eat dogfish flesh, but because of its acid content a way to preserve it had not yet been found. Ways had been tried but the fish would literally eat its way out of the can.

Young Dr. and Mrs. Cook, Elaine and Bill, and the family, Allison, Jonathon, and Heather, were learning the ways and means of island life on the old homestead. They were discovering that the simple life was not so simple and life in the country with fresh cream and milk, homemade bread and butter and garden fresh vegetables is a long-term project, sort of a born-and-bred idea and not to be stepped into lightly.

Margaret Severson's milking days were over. She certainly missed her bossies but she was now free of all the chores of cooling, bottling, straining, and delivering the milk. Those who had enjoyed all her rich milk and cream transferred their patronage to the Norths who had purchased her cow. They were about to name her Jezebel, so possessed of the devil she seemed on her first day in her new surroundings. Things had really been up in the air at the time. It all started when Mardi took a flying leap off the porch and made a crash landing, ending in some colorful though painful bruises. Corky, who we thought to be content to ride in his Model T, had purchased a two-place Aeronca Chief, and, if you could ground him long enough to ask him what he needed a plane for, he would answer, "Oh, it's just another challenge."

It was ironic that no one was around to appreciate Corky's efforts and inventive idea for laying the dust. He was now our new road boss and he rigged up a 250-gallon tank with some perforated pipe. After filling the tank with sea water he spent a whole day sprinkling our dusty roads. Then the rains came and it continued for days.

The coolish dewy mornings and the chirping crickets reminded us that vacation time was over. There was a flurry of activity everywhere as camps and cozy cottages were closing up. The young people were packing and making ready for their schooling and colleges. Our own little red schoolhouse had been scrubbed and polished and the bell in the belfry was ready to ring. Its familiar sound rang out on the clear September air and eleven bright-eyed boys and girls wended their way through woodsy paths and county roads to the cultural center of the island where their mother-teacher team, Lizanne and Mary, continued to mold their young minds, helping them on to schools of higher learning and making them better able to cope with the perplexities of life.

Leave it to the wild geese, they knew when it was time to leave. Never before had there been anything like it on Waldron. On Columbus Day came winds of hurricane force. The roar was deafening and the blasts dynamic—live trees snapped and were uprooted, driven and hurled through the air; barns and roofs collapsed; boats were lifted up and carried away. It whipped up the sea around us into a seething lather and the spindrift, intensified by the moonlight, carried over the land, picking up pebbles and debris, bespattering windows with salt spray, searing and killing the leaves of deciduous trees. The orchards were hard hit and denuded of their winter crop of apples and pears. Then came the rain lashing down, washing the face of the earth, and in the morning everything was serene. Skies were blue with fluffy white clouds and I could imagine a dove flying over with an olive branch in its beak.

It took more than an axe to get us through this one; there were over 300 trees down across the county roads alone. We were grateful for the logging crews with their strong arms and heavy equipment to help clear the way.

Corky North didn't know which might take off next, his house or his plane. Mardi had already taken off for the Seattle Fair with Larry, and Terry was with the Chevs in Friday Harbor so he covered Chet with a pillow in case the windows shattered and spent several hours keeping his plane from taking off, sans the pilot. He hadn't been aware of the fifteen or more big trees which had fallen around the yard, and there were only two or three trees left standing in the orchard. Two other particularly vulnerable spots had been hit, the Magraw's and Weaver's. They were up most of the night barring windows and doors and bracing the roof while treasured and picturesque old cherry trees, madrona, firs, and lombardy poplars snapped and fell to the ground. And there were a few who slept through it all.

Alice McDonald, after a trying time on the mainland, was exhausted. She slept.

Although we were in the lee of the wind, the noise had made me restless. I got up and walked around; I asked Jim, "How hard do you think it is blowing?" Seemingly not alarmed, Jim said simply, "Oh, about ninety. Come to bed and let's get some sleep." So the Loverings slept.

When reviewing the effects of the wind with awe and wonder it reminded me of how helpless we are in the face of the forces of nature. It was quite a show. The porch and part of the roof were torn off from the Gordon's new cabin; their boathouse and tool shed collapsed. Ralph Wood's boathouse washed away. The McDonald's boat was blown from its blocks and had a hole knocked in its hull; their punt was carried away altogether along with an Indian dugout, an old landmark. A tree had fallen on the Tibs' guesthouse. No one was hurt, but the loss of the trees, that was the saddest part of it all. Margaret told of one huge dogwood tree that had fallen while in full bloom (second blooming). She tenderly referred to it as the Old Monarch which had been in the family forever; all the growing children carved their initials in its bark. The spreading madrona tree which graced Helen Ludwig's cabin and which on moonlit nights would appear to be covered with diamonds, was no more. The wayward wind had showed no mercy.

Brothers and sisters, French and Lovering, had given ye olde log postal building its annual facelift and the room was gay with greenery and fresh chrysanthemums garnered from our wind- and rain-battered gardens. The Platter of Plenty (we couldn't find a horn) overflowed with fruits of the harvest. The rest of the good wives were busy preparing two turkey birds and appropriate potages. When all was in readiness we paused awhile to praise God from whom all blessings flow.

We were all saddened by the passing of our friend and old timer Stanley Gale who died in his sleep on December

24, 1962. He was 80 years old, native of England, and served in the English Navy before coming to Canada and the U.S. It was not until his retirement years that Waldron came to know him and we fondly dubbed him *Squire*, tending his sheep and keeping his 40 acres neat and orderly. When it was learned that he had a bad heart, he and his wife, Louise, moved to Seattle. Their daughter, Peggy, and her husband, Joe, closed up the old log cabin with sighs and chuckles evoked by the assortment of stored relics from an era of lace-topped corset covers, divided skirts, and twelve-inch waists. Stanley said the memory of a good life, fresh air, and hard work would help to sustain him to live to a ripe old age.

The old siren of the sea began to stir up my mate's blood again so we went to Seattle where Jim found a berth on the *Canada Mail* and then transferred to the *Java Mail* for the American Mail Line. He would sail as chief navigator and was bound for a three-month trip sailing to the Orient, Japan, and India. We had an interesting two weeks together before he sailed. The sun also rises in Seattle, reflecting its roseate glow over the tall buildings as the heart of the city gradually awakens. We enjoyed the throbbing pulse of the crowds; the streams of cars stopping and going; pedestrians, walk, wait, and don't walk; the spirit of St. Valentine in the store windows; and the colorful Pike Street Market. "Beauty is in the eye of the beholder," and best of all was in the city at night with its thousand and one twinkling lights, a city hushed and at rest.

Rat race, space race, human race—I wonder where we are all going. Wherever it is, I hope there will be a few little Waldrons left to come back to.

Chapter Sixteen
Flood Tide
1963-1964

Suddenly it was spring again—the hummingbirds at their feeders or flitting from blossom to blossom, gold-finches swinging low on the tall grasses, pigeons in the cherry trees and caterpillars in their tents and those greedy intruders, the starlings. Such a noise they made! No threat of a silent spring here.

In this ever-changing world we can be sure of nature repeating its miracles but what of man? Can we keep our island simplicity—our picturesque old barns and old world lamps, rustic little out-buildings and little red schoolhouse? This was the problem confronting the members of the school board who met at Corky and Mardi's to discuss the re-roofing of the school building; whether to use split shakes, asbestos shingles, or the new aluminum sheeting. Would sentiment and feeling for our rustic setting be taken into consideration or would the speed and ease of handling the more modern materials be the choice? There should be a happy medium, somewhere.

The Norths seemed to have found a happy medium; a most modern house in a super rustic setting, a most modern aluminum combination barn, hangar, and garage which housed the cow on one side, Corky's plane on the other side. Surely this was an example of the new co-existing with the old. But what of bossy's feelings? Would she rebel at this winged intrusion or could she live in harmony with it? Only time would tell and it might also heal the raw, naked wounds of the bulldozer where the new airstrip had taken shape on what was once a beloved pastoral scene.

The school board met again at Juniper Cove Ranch to

work out the preliminary budget for the 1963-64 school year. It was hard for Bob Weaver to settle down to per-diem equalization with seagulls swooping down for a supper of herring right under his nose, or for Corky to concentrate on building maintenance with planes tipping their wings as they flew over. Mardi said she would draw the blinds but we all knew there were no such things on Waldron. Back to the roof; we found it to be too high or rather the budget too low. We were thinking of having an old-time roofing bee.

Summer seemed to be off to a good start with good "girl watching" as one announcer put it. The swimming was great; so invigorating when you came out, they told me. The bouffant beauties of the city arrive in contrast with our long-haired lassies, and the teen scene teemed with activity. The *Freya Dora* had her posterior scraped and painted ready for another season of graceful sailings. The young 'uns paddled their canoes and the tall ones ventured out to the rocks for abalone and rock cod. Oysters and clam bakes, wiener roasts, sleeping bags, bed shacks, and pup tents. Ain't vacation grand!

Norman C. McDonald said he was the busiest man on the island, digging worms for the robins and making a tricycle for his 5- to 7½-horsepower twin-screw cruiser. His middle "C" must surely stand for charming as it was just that to pass the time of day with Mac and Alice, to visit their home and sip some of Alice's Old Nettle '62 or lemon verbena tea, or to watch the birds come to her sanctuary to feed and dabble in the bird bath. Alice had a new hob-by—growing old-world herbs to enhance her cookery, to attract our feathered friends, and to add to rose petals and lavender for potpourri to delight the senses and which, she claimed, also had power to renew the spirit. My spirits would be renewed (not that I did much moping around) when Jim returned safely after one of his long voyages. He was back on the island after successfully navigating the *Java Mail* through the waters of the Far East, carrying a mixed cargo of Bulgar wheat, oil, and a few artificially inseminated pigs. They had just missed the cyclone and tidal wave that wiped out thousands in Pakistan. Those who had been worrying about a sugar shortage could take heart—I had a little inside dope, Jim brought back 900 tons of it.

Turnabout is fair play. It was the Island Sky Ferries, or an important part of it, which was put in our care when the Franklins, Roy, and Margaret Ann, Steve, Nancy, Susan, Janet, and Kenny, were set loose and fancy free on our shores for 24 hours. Coming from Friday Harbor in the *Speedy Gonzales* they were made comfortable in Margaret Severson's beach cabin. When the natives heard of this state of affairs, the tribal drums went into action, the fish were alerted, and runners were sent out to call in the clans for a pow-wow chow at Helen Ludwig's cabin. Cakes and goodies were hurriedly popped into the oven, old cider brought up from the cellar, and the coffee pot was put on. The press was frankly perplexed when the guests of honor arrived, as I had confused them with another Franklin family who were really not Franklins at all but Johnsons. It would take too long to explain but the *real* Franklins were initiated to one phase of island society.

The following day they were up bright and early and out catching rock cod and creating a foaming wake, zipping around the island. The girls were having a great time riding the Magraw's horse while Margaret Ann was turned loose in my raspberry patch. They left again in the company cruiser which Roy called part of the company's physical fitness program.

Everyone was talking about it, everyone was excited about it, and almost everyone was doing it. The fishing fever was rampant and I guess you just haven't lived until you have felt that tug on your line, the expectancy and thrill of reeling in a fighting silver beauty. Avid anglers all around were out there pitching and tossing with the whim of the wind and the tides—big boats and little boats, sail boats and row boats. From three pounds to thirty, the feeling of pride in your fish was the same.

Even the youthful crew of the *Freya Dora* had taken a hand in it when Susie felt a strike. Steve reeled it in. Julie netted it just as the leader broke. Then Kathy gaffed it just as the bottom of the net fell out. Steve had caught a twelve-pounder and this one was ten pounds, so what better to do with two fishes than to feed the multitude. These generous teenagers called in the clans and shared their fishes at a salmon bake.

Chuck and Mildred Ludwig had little concern for angling but enjoyed their tasty morsel with a little of the staff of life. Their pride and joy was the windmill they were raising which was a bright landmark from Cowlitz Bay. Rain or shine, Dr. and Mrs. Ludwig never lost their zest for island living and were regular vacationers here, working on their plans to build and planting trees. Chuck had received his Ph.D. in organic chemistry in 1961 and was now employed as a research chemist at the Puget Sound Pulp and Timber Company in Bellingham while Mildred was teaching kindergarten at Lowell School.

Cameras were clicking in the early morning sunshine as six prim and peppy people in their simple suits boarded the plane for Bellingham. After using up over a half mile of Coates Corded cotton and treadling the old Singer sewing machine for weeks, Lizanne Magraw and her five girls, Allison, Kristy, Linnea, Melanie, and Martha were waved on their way to St. Paul, Minnesota, to attend a family reunion of Jack's folks, sisters and brothers, and their progeny.

It was a sure sign of rain when road boss North started using the road grader and preparing the ditches for the winter precipitation. Corky was a man of many facets. He was then contemplating another iron in the fire, as he negotiated with Bob Schoen to take over the ferry, *Nordland*. He had in mind a plan to modify the superstructure and be on a daily call basis for inter-island freight and ferry service.

For Fran and Bill Chevalier a fresh new line of little white squares was flying in the breeze as another little fisherman joined the family. Their fourth child, Mitchell Edward, was born on September 26. The Grams and Grammas Chevalier and Lovering were having their day too, taking turns with their little charges, Cindy, Bucky (Matt), and Marty. "Careful now! Watch it! Whatever you do, don't." If you don't think you can get a charge from two-, three-, and four-year-olds with their refreshing, beguiling, inquiring, and teasing ways, well, take it from a reliable source, you can.

Seemed like a little late in the season for taking a vacation but as Sam and Agnes Fleming put it, it is always the season for coming to Waldron. And, as the heart grows a little older, the autumn of the year is probably more appealing with its less intoxicating and more tranquil scenes. The Flemings, who were the grandparents of six, felt like millionaires; their five-acre swatch of Sandy Point was the beginning of their mansion among a few remaining virgin firs.

I can still picture my father as he would stand by the window saying, "Blow, San Antonio, blow, breaketh the mast, splitteth the sail." SE, SW, NE, NW, it had circled the globe, churning up the sea into an angry fury, littering the beaches, making bargain days for beachcombers, and a gold mine for organic gardeners who valued seaweed as a complete fertilizer. The beaches had been so thick. Then the rain, how it poured—2.4 inches in one day! It was such a relief for those who had reached the spit bath stage and for some who were wringing out the few drops off the roof. Oh, the simple joys of island living! We were washing our hair in soft water again. The rain barrel was full.

Anything that I may have to report for that fateful week in November would have been trivial and trite in the face of the great tragedy which struck the heart and homes of the nation—the cruel, shameless indignity to all we hold dear in the American way of life; the assassination of our beloved leader, President John F. Kennedy. We on Waldron grieved along with the rest of the world and his bereaved family for the loss of this great man.

"We never know, we never know." How often had these words been repeated. Because of sickness and the gravity of recent events, the school program, the highlight of our island festivities, was omitted that year. But Christmas would have been sad indeed without the carol singing, and with all the young folk home for the holidays there was a good chorus of voices to go a-wassailing. The night was fair with a wisp of a moon occasionally peeking through the drifting clouds, and the mainland lights could be seen shining across the dark waters as we made the rounds.

There wasn't any fig pudding but there were hot beverages, cookies, and a warm welcome by each fireside as the glad tidings were repeated. We like to believe it was the same spirit that brought the Bellingham *Christmas Ship* to our shores across those stormy waters, despite the pitching and the mal-de-mer. The music rang out their greeting as Santa and the children huddled in the dock shed sheltered from the lashing rain, receiving gifts. While the clowns made a valiant try at fulfilling their role, balloons were whipped away, bobbing across the water. Thus man's labor of love floated to the beach and found its way into our homes.

When Jim started to pace the deck I knew the time had come for the parting of the ways and for the replenishment of the family fortune. Shipping was still in a slump, and for a seaman to be without a ship was like being a man without a country. Since the Olympic S.S. Co. had folded up, Jim's only recourse was to add his name to the list at the Masters, Mates, and Pilots union hall. I went along with him to Seattle and we took a little hotel apartment where I could cook for him. We had to count our nickels and Jim would haunt the hiring hall every morning at 10 a.m. and I would be a roving reporter again, seeing a few glimpses on the other side of the fence.

Perky little pigeons strutted and gray gulls glided over the roof tops, ever watchful for the tidbits left on the surrounding window sills. Inside these gray walls, one flower in a pot was a garden and the cooking was instant and packaged. Which brings to mind one young boy, hungrily sniffing around the kitchen when he came home from school and saying, "Oh, goody, I smell a package cake." A far cry from grandma's day.

We had been in Seattle for over two weeks when it came. Jim was transfigured and seemed to walk a little taller. It was only a third mate's job, but from then on we threw all caution to the wind and dined in the best restaurants. The sky was the limit. Such is the life of a sailorman, either a feast or a famine.

Jim sailed on the S.S. *Hawaiian Planter* for the Matson Navigation Company bound for another voyage to India, and I was soon back on the island with the cool soft earth under my feet, the Madrona tree over my head, and the profound stillness all about me. So remote from the bright, pulsating world of speed, symphonies, and extravaganzas from which I had returned.

With the coming the *Mr. ZIP*, the Post Office department was going all out for full speed ahead in the movement of the mails. The *Marine Commuter*, the next boat to be on the mail run, carried passengers but no freight. This situation sort of left us out on a limb and we were not very happy about it.

Corky and his popular little craft, *Nordland*, had our problem of heavy freight under control, and Billy, with the *Service*, helped with the bringing of supplies. He and his dad blew in alongside the dock bringing the first load of trees for Phil's arboretum; magnolias for magnificence, dogwood and oak for shade, apple trees to sit under; peach, pear, and plum. Phil really meant business. Arthur Murphy was his landscape architect in New York and Messieurs Burn and Weaver his Waldron consultants. There was a fever of activity as native trees were felled, brush cleared and burned to make way for fencing, and ground was prepared for an orchard, lawns, ornamental trees, and shrubs. A few eastern ideas transplanted to the west. Who said, "Never the twain would meet"?

Digger Weaver had to keep his foot to the grindstone as he made his holes in the ground; he dug them wide and he dug them deep, didn't believe in making a fifty cent hole for a five dollar tree. About fifty more trees followed; filberts and chestnuts, golden rain and golden chain trees, Mimosa, Albizzia, Julibrissin, Cephaletaxux, Liquid Amber Stryacifulus. Pardon me, no speeky the Eengleesh.

Sometimes when my mate was gone and I was left with all my modern conveniences that needed pampering, gassing, and oiling and so often refusing to function, I felt like packing my bag and giving it all back to the Indians.

Time was when I could pick up my pole and take off to a secluded rock and quietly meditate while dangling for cod and my problems would melt away. Now the otters would be there first, they would sit there on their rock making funny little noises while munching on my fish. Maybe otters have problems too; I heard that someone was after their skin.

It was the kind of story we could tell the grandchildren, how, in spite of gale-force winds and mountainous seas the mailboat came through. After this episode we had a good deal more respect for the operators of the *Marine Commuter* that, without a doubt, had proved her seaworthiness. We would like to think it was sheer courage and a desire to serve rather than foolhardiness that brought them out on that wild March morning when they could have come the following day. We wanted to give credit where credit was due, for bravely attempting to land the mail with all odds against them. Knowing full well that it was unlikely they would come, we had huddled closer to the old iron stove at the post office discussing the situation. As the wind blew stronger, our appetites increased as we anticipated the days without our supply of groceries. Yet we still scanned the horizon in hopes.

We were just about ready to give up and go home when someone cried, "It's coming! I see it!" And there she was in a trough, throwing a spume that would rival any sea. The moments which followed were filled with anxiety for them as they made repeated tries to land the mail while being pitched and tossed in the furious sea. They finally succeeded. I was sure that a little prayer went up for them when they took off, seemingly swallowed up and lost to sight. As Roy Crum used to say, "And that's true, too." It may seem a little melodramatic but you have to appeal to their imagination if you tell it to the grandkids.

The members of the school board had their heads together again estimating revenues and attendance for the 1964-65 school year. It had been eight pupils, one educational unit, remote school, equalization, and state apportionments. They reviewed with pride the accomplishment of the year; the new roof, a chair for the teacher, the world globe, and a new double-barreled stove. They touched on the possibility of indoor facilities. With the County Sanitarian, Bob Weaver, as a member of the board, we thought it was bound to come. In the meantime, the moving and re-roofing of the present little WPA-vintage cubicles were discussed.

Speaking of sanitation recalls to mind a little practice in England. When I was a girl, the milkman made his house-to-house deliveries in a horse-drawn cart. He would ladle the sweet, whole milk from large open cans, filling the jugs and pitchers, gills, pints, and quarts left on the doorstep of those who wished it. When he was gone and we were sure that no one was looking, we would run out and swiftly shovel up the horse deposit for our garden. Now horticulturists on Waldron could appreciate the value of this fast diminishing commodity, but it could well make sanitarians raise a disapproving eyebrow.

In that age of think-big mergers and consolidation, it was rumored that the days of the one-room school were numbered, but to prove that it was still the heart of our island community, the old bell in the belfry rang out loud and clear to summon folks to the spring program. As though to reassure us that we were not ready to give over to the rats, teacher Lizanne Magraw had conjured up a delightfully original little playlet, well spiced with humor and satire for our enjoyment. Her nine pupils, turned rats for the occasion, displayed their usual charm and freshness as they gnawed and scampered about, revealing some interesting and personal facts from the school's history and records which stirred fond memories and many chuckles from the audience.

Beatrice Baer said that she had found a cure for lonesomeness that worked. She would hang a coffee cup on the limb of a tree nearby and wait. The Weavers bit on her bait which lured them into her lair and whiled away many a pleasant afternoon. For a newcomer to the fold she caught on fast. It must have been the gypsy in her soul and the beat of the flamenco music she played, for the young people flocked to her. That was how another music practice group for guitar only was born.

The scoop of the year was when Bob and Mary Weaver learned that their son, Andy, was accepted at Yale University with a handsome grant and generous provisions. Andy was an exceptionally gifted young man, deeply interested in human relations and literature.

While I was in San Francisco meeting the Mate, I gathered another little gem of "local boy makes good" news. North Burn, son of our departed (to Florida) friends, June and Farrar, was appointed Vice President and Secretary of Mills College in Oakland.

Another little news item of distinction came from my sister, Madge. She was made a member of the most exclusive club in the world for her prowess on the golf course. She made a hole-in-one at Harding Park. Should I add that the odds are 25,000 to one? Madge was in training here last summer, climbing the mountain and on the working end of a clam shovel.

On his return to the States, Jim reported fair weather and smooth sailing. I joined him in San Francisco, being swooshed 15,000 feet into the atmosphere, floating on downy clouds, and looking down on rivers and lakes and big cones while traveling 450 miles an hour. It was quite stupendous for a country gal. It was thrilling to see the familiar sights and sounds of the mighty rollers and surf crashing against the Seal Rocks, and the big liners going toward the Golden Gate Bridge while dining at the famous Cliff House with Jim and my five sisters. How the city scene had changed with the human tidal wave. The once quiet rolling hills were now covered with wall-to-wall overpasses and ramps that replaced the ferry building and the colorful flower stands that used to greet you. Now instead of the scent of violets it is the aroma of Hills Brothers coffee that fills the nostrils as you drive over the Oakland Bay Bridge.

After Jim's carefree life on the bounding main, where the only tools he used were a sextant and a pencil to make his calculations, he found life on Waldron rather exhausting. Chores, chopping wood, and the hassle of gas barrels took some getting used to, but then his times ashore were usually quite brief.

Ray and Mary Tiberghien celebrated their fiftieth wedding anniversary on June 7, 1964, at a reception given by their nieces. The air was sweet with the scent of roses plucked from the island gardens to complement nature's bounteous beauty of sand and sandflat which surrounded their door, and the sun couldn't help shining down on this very special occasion when over 70 people, including islanders and off-island families and friends, came to congratulate them.

Mary had been an expert horsewoman and liked to drive the sulkies, exercising the horses, sitting on their tails while driving them in reverse. As Ray would say, "She was a caution." She was the prettiest girl in town and he, the handsomest man, so they were married at the Tiberghien farm home in Sac City, Iowa, on June 5, 1914.

Subsequently, Ray got into the Postal Service in Lytton, Iowa, as a mail carrier and was transferred to Bellingham in 1926. Here they had a showplace on Chuckanut Drive where Mary's love for a garden flourished. Their union was not blessed with a family but they had a host of adoptions, being loved and admired by all ages. Ray was uncle to many little families on his mail route, sharing their secret joys and sorrows as he watched them grow. They had laid up no great material treasures on earth but there was ample to live in comfortable simplicity on Waldron and to do a little traveling together after Ray retired in 1942.

Mary wore a tawny orchid corsage and Ray wore lipstick of many hues; he was 83 years old and still in his heyday, loving the admiration of the fair sex and still warbling out love songs to Mary, his own true love for 50 years.

Norman McDonald said, "I made it to 80, now I'm going to try for a hundred." The celebration was wide and varied. He listened to his favorite music as we wined and dined him; he picnicked on the beach with his family, Gary and Norma from Lummi; he was serenaded at the post office and again at the Frenches by a chorus of young voices with guitar accompaniment. While this was going on he was being sought out by some other admirers who had prepared his favorite chocolate cake, a he-man cake made from scratch and decorated with the simple inscription of "MAC 1964 A.T." It was so simple it stumped the experts.

Another birthday rolled around for Margaret Severson on the 14th. She said she had never had any desire to travel to the usual far-off places but her one wish was to see Alaska some day. Her wish was about to come true as she waved her jet plane round-trip ticket, which was a birthday gift from her son, Ab. She joined him for a trip on the ferry *Matanuska*, a fishing trip in Ab's own boat, and saw more salmon than you can imagine. Margaret returned with a camera full of shots and a keg full of salmon.

Cindy said, "But grandma, the flowers don't need another drink of water." That was a five-year old's logic and, confidentially, my philosophy had been wearing thin. We seemed to have an unusual amount of summer precipitation; if we weren't basking in the sunshine, we were singing in the rain. Billy was bringing in the bacon while fishing in Alaska. Fran and her Chevalier cherubs and Nash cousins made the most of their vacation on the beach.

Oh, ye olde Indian Summer, no wonder they write songs about it. In England they call it St. Augustine's summer when it occurs in September but no matter what the legend, it was wonderful; that indefinable aura in the atmosphere, the hazy sunshine, the fiery red sunsets, and the smouldering afterglow. Dr. Ludwig says it is the dust particles in the air that cause the fantastic color.

It was all so hushed and still, and but for the crows and gulls, I had begun to think that the island was deserted until the *Nordland's* whistle jolted me out of my reverie and I knew then, by the banging of the barrels on the beach, that it was Monday and that a new work week was about to begin when the sheep buyers drove their trucks ashore. Later in the day Phil arrived and after the initial amenities he lost no time making the rounds of his plantation which he viewed with mixed emotions. He was amazed at the growth of the native willows, wild roses, blackberry, and snowberry. He made a quick deduction that willows must grow an inch daily while some of the transplants only that much in a month or more. On the whole he was much enthused but decided he was no match for the willows after hacking and slashing at them in the rain.

Three mysterious green lights could be seen shining across the waters from the shores of Cowlitz Bay, standing out like sentinels in the night. No strange rendezvous here, smuggling, or burning the midnight oil. It was simply the parking lights of the commercial herring boat fleet, relieving the waters of hundreds of tons of herring. It was an interesting operation and at one time when I was fishing for a story I rowed out, waiting for them to make a haul. It would have made such a pretty picture, all that silver glittering in the sunset, but they kept moving around and finally took off. Bob Weaver rowed out one time, too, and he got his pictures with some herring to boot. He just happened to have a wash tub in the boat–pretty cagey.

Elvida Johnson had a way too and a good recipe for canning pickled herring. Bob Weaver had other ways and means of extracting things. He could grow eight to ten pounds of potatoes to a vine, cabbages bigger than footballs, and such carrots! One of them alone would feed a family of four. It must have been that old quack grass and seaweed compost and being a patient man. He tried an experiment, covering an area with plastic for some months until it had simply rotted out and then spreading it with seaweed and letting it set awhile. When he dug it in the spring, he had the richest, blackest soil and I was green with envy.

For many moons the restless spirits of Waldron had longed to shake the shackles of ghostly tradition, to dispense with the fol-de-rol and misty raiment of the past and to have just a quiet little barbecue on the beach. The devil himself lent a hand to dig the pit and hoist the spit and started the small inferno with all his little imps in attendance. A nice fatted sheep had been chosen and dressed for the occasion and for eight hours the aroma of roast mutton wafted across the moors. It was simply out of this world! All the Waldron wives had concocted special brews and magical menus, dill rolls, garlic bread, salads, pies, and hot spiced cider.

Chapter Seventeen
The Mail Flies Through
1965-1966

"Halloa out there! And a misty morning to you from behind the island curtain." It had been foggy for days: first it's here, then it isn't; now you see us, now you don't...and out of the nebulas came a new pastime for Citizens' Band fans, *fog watching.* Anyone could join in the act, reporting to Island Sky Ferries if the fog was low, high, drifting, or the island really socked in.

There was nothing much else going on but if you were the aggressive and outdoor type and liked clams there were some minus tides in the early evening hours. It was pretty eerie out there on the beach with the full moon trying to penetrate the gray mists and the banshee at Turn Point Light moaning out its warning to the deep-throated whistle of the ocean liners passing in the night. You could work off some of your caloric intake of Christmas and, what is more, it was fun spotting those rectangular holes by lantern light, bending and digging. Your reward was great; that rich, hot chowder or steamers with garlic butter.

It was nice weather for ducks; the copious precipitation in February caused a bit of a problem on the roads which in places were inundated. Mr. Road Boss had been out with his shovel digging ditches and clearing culverts. Mrs. Road Boss exclaimed, as she hurried into the post office, "I lost an oar where the Mississippi runs into the Missouri." Mardi was such a card and could keep things lively with her little innuendos helping you forget the dismal, depressing drip.

There was a great remembering when, and catching up on the years between, when Mrs. Edna Finley revisited the island after 32 years. She had first come as Edna Boone in

1922 to teach school and then later as Mrs. Finley with her young son, Bernard, who attended school here with Carol Severson, Alice Johnson, North and Bobby Burn, and Betty and Margie Chevalier. She wanted to see her old stomping grounds, the little cottage, and the new tile floor and aluminum roof on the schoolhouse. To her surprise she noted the quaint little outbuildings were still there. She recalled how Charlie Fahlstrom had brought water for her in a wheelbarrow in five-gallon cans. Her son, Bernard, was now a practicing doctor of psychiatry in Los Angeles and Edna told a funny story about him once occupying a sanitary couch, a donation to the cause from Frank Graignic. Seems young Bernard couldn't sleep very well on it but Frank's dog had no trouble. They had to burn the mattress.

For the sake of the younger generation, maybe I should elucidate a little about the couch; perhaps they would know it better as a cot, or what a trundle bed would be to my grandmother. And, if you are wondering why they had to burn the mattress, well, it is sort of a shaggy-dog story. The end I leave to your imagination.

The birds really startled me when I encountered them at the sawmill corner. There isn't any sawmill anymore; the war broke out and it fell into disuse. Like Charlie's road, it wasn't really his; just the name and association still sticks. Oh! Jim would get real perturbed when I would go traipsing off like this instead of getting to the point; it was his training aboard ship. He would say that when he wanted an order carried out he couldn't weave a fairy story around it before he gave a command. "Aye, aye, sir, hard a port."

Now, where was I? About to tell you of the birds and peacocks. Marjorie French had been gathering data, what things they like to eat, and to her dismay she discovered they liked comfrey; they had eaten all the plants she had set out. Comfrey, in case you are wondering, is an old-world herb used to congeal wounds. It has great medicinal powers. A concoction of its mucilaginous root is used in making cough syrup. It is beneficial to humans and animals alike, so peacocks are not the dumb, rather useless creatures one might think. Oh, those male tail feathers certainly added a rainbow of color to the countryside.

It was just the day before it happened that "Mac," who was a great source of wisdom on Waldron, commented rather cynically, "If the fall-out doesn't get you then the earthquake will." Well, it didn't exactly get us but surely something was rocking the boat, and we were a little shaken. Marjorie French said she was a little seasick from the motion. Lizzie Chevalier, who heard the eerie sound and saw the back porch shaking, thought, "Now, what is Bill starting the washing machine for?" The early birds at the school said the chairs were waltzing around and the flag pole and the belfry tower were waving back and forth. A wall clock stopped at the Weaver's. Elvida Johnson feared that she would never sleep in her lovely new bedroom which was almost complete. Mardi North was up at the barn milking the cow, hummm! At 8:30? It was 5:30 a.m. in my day. Anyway, it nearly knocked her off the stool. The airplane was banging around in the next stall, the barn was shaking, and even the cow was having a tremor. I think Margaret Severson was about the only one who was unaware of anything happening; she was out feeding her livestock or honeying up the hummingbirds. Such a flock of them!

God bless Grandfather! He remembered us in his will. Whereas, funds from regular sources within the county fell far short of the estimated needs of School District No. 21 and whereas, the new formula from legislative session extraordinaire for state apportionments was inadequate to supplement the 1965-66 Waldron School Budget, the members of the board have determined that a state of emergency exists. Therefore, a resolution had been made that a special school election be requested to vote upon an 18-mill levy. Signed—but just as the pen was lifted, word came from County Superintendent Carl White, to hold it. Someone came up with the grandfather clause which saved us from the revenuers. Everyone was happy that our little elementary center of learning could carry on, that the teacher would not have to take a cut in salary, that no further burden be made on local taxpayers, and that the sagging schoolhouse steps could be repaired and new roofs put on the old *New Deal* outhouses.

Instead of sittin' and knittin' I had been flittin' again, meeting the mate of the *Canada Mail* returning from her maiden voyage to the Orient. Jim reported a fine trip, which could encompass anything from monsoons to mutiny. After saying howdy to the folks here, Jim headed for Friday Harbor to work on his own boat, the *Fifty-Fifty*. Billy had sold the *Service*, which was now too small for its crew of little helpers. This is where the *Sharon Linda* made her debut. Billy converted her into a gillnetter and family boat and we all went on a trial run.

There was a little launching party at the Burn's Lumber, Engine, And Boat (BLEAB)-works. It was a work of art that Bob built for his young son, Mark, fashioned entirely of beach-combed oddments of red cedar, Alaska cedar, and fir, which he had sawed into strips and planks, molded and chipped and shaped into a round-bottomed double-ender. Spirits were high in spite of the wind and rain squalls. There were tense moments as Bob stood shivering on the brink, trying to hold the craft, while Lisa held a bottle of poor man's champagne poised over the bow, while a decision was being made whether the words she would utter should be, "I christen thee *No Name*" or, "I pronounce thee *Seaworthy*." I thought she would never make the break, the words were lost to the winds, but the break was clean and right on the mark and the *No Name* made her debut midst cheers from the beach, riding out on the water like a graceful white gull.

Doe was in a state of high elation after months and months with her nose to the creative grindstone. She had completed the drawings for her children's book, *Andrew Henry's Meadow*, which was to be published in the very near future. She was now able to spread her wings a little and went to visit her mother. Her father, Lage Wernstedt, died in 1959, and her mother, Adele (Dottie), was remarried to Walter Graham and they continued to live on a little farm on Guemes Island.

June was a perfect month, hay all cut and in the barn, and the sheep sheared. It was a gardener's world—new peas and baby beets in the pot; roses, poppies, and pinks; thrips, aphids, spider mites, mildew, beetles, weevils, and lace bugs; robins, pigeons, and crows. "Dear, dear, and . . . Oh, my!"; it was also a child's world. Kool-aid and Band-aid, bumps and bruises, wa-wa and wocks, wieners, whistles and sand in the sandwich.

A bunch of us oldies were on the beach reminiscing over our schooldays and vacation jobs and some interesting facts unfolded. Elvida Johnson told us of having worked in a sleeping bag factory, they had to wear masks. Doe Burn had worked in the salmon cannery, sliming fish. I told of working in a biscuit factory, separating paper cups for the chocolate packers. Mardi North had waited tables and made signs for the Odd Fellows dance on Orcas. Lizanne Magraw was very reluctant to tell of her experience working for a costume designer, but from what I did gather, I put together that he was a tyrant. He was now a big shot in Hollywood. I also told them of the strict regimentation of the girls' school I had attended in England, how those of us who were late would have to march around the hall while my sister, Ethel, played a drone's march on the piano. I had been given a smart box on the ear for having a smirk on my face.

Emory Johnson, who had gone to school in Sweden, recalled having to trek six miles every day on racing skis. He told of some old time discipline wherein the young offender was told to go cut his own birch rod, then got it where it hurt the most. But it hadn't helped, he went right on tearing the girls' blouses. Elvida had us in stitches with her Swedish tongue twister which, when translated meant, "Seven thousand, seven-hundred, and seventy-seven seasick seamen." You really should try it sometime.

Bob and Mary Weaver told a group of us about a sea monster raising its ugly head while they were fishing around Pt. Disney. They noticed a brown object in the water and thinking it to be a deadhead went about their business. An hour or so later they got a closer look and the thing was breathing. It had a hideous head with eyes giving them the cold stare. It was hard to describe the massive projection of muscle, this cow- or horse-like head about 30 inches long. This was no mythical sea serpent with undulating tail. When it submerged it went straight down. It had given them the shudders and they kept their distance, but they were curious, thinking it to be some sort of seal. I did a little research and identified it as the Northern Elephant Seal. This one must have been a male—the bulls grow to be 5,000 pounds and have a trunk-like extension of nose which can be expanded. They come up on the beaches in the winter and spring to shed their skins and even though they are harmless, I'd hate to come face to face with one changing his clothes on my beach. Bill and Billy Chevalier had seen one one time off Candelabra Point. Bill had thrown up his arms in horror!

Years ago a couple were out jigging for cod and snagged an octopus. It too was a repulsive denizen of the deep, measuring ten feet from arm-tip to arm-tip, and each tentacle was equipped with numerous suction cups which, although the thing was dead, reached out to grab onto things. It was coral in color and had one eye and a beak like a parrot. Part of it is supposed to be edible. Ever hear of octopie? There would have to be two of them for that, or would it be octopusses?

Jim whisked away again, bringing to an end his two-week interlude between ships. His home away from home for the next three and a half months was again the S.S.

Java Mail. Being the ship's navigator, he set his courses for Ketchikan and Kobe, S. Vietnam, Malaysia, East Pakistan, and India. In the meantime, I did a little globe trotting, rubbing shoulders with some ancestral ghosts, sipping typical English tea in a typical English town and traipsing with the tourists when I went to Victoria, B.C., with my two sisters, Geva and Marian. We saw a replica of Anne Hathaway's cottage and a bit of old England at Chaucer Lane where we had crumpets and tea in a staid old atmosphere. We learned some interesting facts about thatched cottages and slept in quaint old canopied beds. These canopies were originally used for the purpose of keeping out drafts, or mice and bugs, which were wont to fall from the thatch. They had no ceilings in the upper stories way back then.

We went on a tour of the Butchart Gardens, "oh"-ing and "ah"-ing as we tiptoed through the petunias and bumped into each other with umbrellas. Oh, jolly! It was just a garden in the rain, but it was lovely.

Time again for the school bell to ring; Lizanne was back at her desk while eight shiny-bright little boys and girls made their way swinging their lunch pails down our dusty roadways in eager anticipation.

I had been busy wielding the paint brush brightening things up and I had fallen for the new fad. Now the phony oak piano was a phony white which met with the approval of the adults, but I was not sure whether the children appreciated this touch of 17th Century drawing room decor. I promised them I wouldn't touch their desks; happiness is a comfortable oaken two-seater.

It was the season for mushrooms and I used to be mad about them until last fall when I nearly poisoned Jim. He was crazy about them also and he was a little miffed when I didn't get around to fixing a bucketful he had picked, but they had all turned black and were full of maggots. Thinking to make it up to him, I surreptitiously left the house, tripped across the meadow to the edge of the woods, and there they were, all pale and pink and plump, just pushing up through the leaf mold. I wasn't greedy. I just picked a bowlful and hurried back before he missed me. After quietly washing and peeling them, I presented them to Jim saying, "There, Darling, I knew you felt bad about the others." Next morning at breakfast I was slicing them into the melted butter when I detected a peculiar effluvia and noticed that they were not cooking up nice and tender as meadow mushrooms should. So I said, "Darling, I hate to discourage you, but I don't like the smell of these mushrooms." I put a few on his plate, leaving mine empty; he just nibbled on them half-heartedly saying I had spoiled his appetite with all my remarks. After about two hours, he said, "Mama, I don't feel so good," and he didn't look so good either, as the few mushrooms he had eaten made him very sick. I rushed over to the expert, Mary Weaver, and she identified the mushrooms as *Agaricus silvicola*, a type to be avoided.

When we first came to the island, Ethan Allen introduced us to the big yellow boletus. He sauteed a skilletful in melted butter into which he added a whole can of evaporated milk; it was very rich. Most mushrooms do not need any gilding—their flavor is unique.

In those days the island abounded in savory fungi, and Margaret Severson remembered that the Japanese used to come over and pick them by the gunnysack full. We discovered fifteen edible varieties, the most common of which was the meadow mushroom, which appears after the first rains in the fall. The morel arrives in the springtime. Others are the purple russula, shaggy manes, scull caps, and puff balls. Even the pesty little fairy ring which grows in the lawn is edible. I am not an authority on these things, but if you know your sporophores and agaricales or lycoperdales, you can pick yourself a dainty dish.

Flash Gordon had sold his place (formerly belonging to Jack Allen) to Walter Abel of Solduc Lands, Inc., and Mr. Abel paid the island a visit. From what I gathered he was planning to build a hunting lodge and a resort of a sort for escapists who want to get away from the maddening crowds. I wondered what Jack Allen would think, if he were alive, to know that his place had been resold for $91,000. At one time he had offered it to Jim for $6,000, lock, stock, and barrel. How values do change! We were asking ourselves, will a supermarket raise its ugly head where once the friendly old barn used to stand? Some gardeners were glomming onto the old hay with glee for mulching. Think of the sweat and brawn that had gone into erecting those weather- and time-worn old buildings in an era when men and women had to really work to eke out a living on the land.

Everything had been up in the air after fire broke out on the current mailboat, the Marine Commuter. Ed Schibig, the skipper, discovered it as he was rounding Neck Point after leaving Friday Harbor. He extinguished the blaze and then it was found that one engine was inoperable. They proceeded to Anacortes on one engine. Later that night another fire started; it was found by Steve Homer, president of the company that had the mail contract. He called the fire department and the damages were estimated to be in the thousands of dollars. Negotiations were started immediately to secure another boat as it was figured it would be at least a month before the Commuter would be back in service.

There are always two sides to any situation and the fire on the mailboat put the post office officials in a predicament. Given such short notice, they were unsuccessful in finding a boat and operator to replace the Commuter, so they hired Tom Wilson of Skyline Air in Anacortes to fly the first class mail to the islands until the existing contract ended on June 30, 1966. Parcel-post was sent by ferry and that was to be the end of our mail and freight boat life-line and the beginning of a new era in our life style.

By the spring of '66, the post office department had decided that aircraft service was the only way to handle the mail. Complaints were no longer coming in about delays and poor service. It was proposed for the first time in island history to offer the mail contract to aircraft only.

Island Sky Ferries (ISF), operating in the islands for some 17 years, determined to bid on the July 1966 mail contract. However, the postal service still held some doubts that airplanes could do a satisfactory job, especially if the islands were to experience a real stormy winter, so instead of a four-year contract they proposed to let it out on a 30-day agreement basis.

For either Skyline or Island Sky to take on the full responsibility of a year-round mail contract would mean more planes and pilots but no bank would loan money for these things on a 30-day contract. Tom Wilson and Roy Franklin, although running competitive flying companies, put their heads together and came up with a plan whereby they could jointly carry the mail by pooling their men and machines so that it wouldn't be necessary to finance additional equipment. They formed a new jointly-owned corporation which they named Island Mail, Inc., and under this title they bid on the contract and got it.

I had just been buzzed; now time was that when you heard that familiar roar it meant just one thing, Roy Franklin was about to drop a message. He was a master at it, never missing his target. But now, thinking it to be Tom Wilson of Skyline Air bringing the mail an hour early, it almost caused a panic. I grabbed what mail there was, sacked it up, and made a dash for the airfield, all the way in low (had no go-power in drive) stopping to collect mail along the way declaring, "The mail's in." It reminded me of Paul Revere warning that the British were coming. It turned out to be Mr. H. M. Byrum, director of the Transportation Division of the Post Office Department, who was arriving to talk over the temporary airlift.

When the new company, Island Mail, Inc., received the contract, Roy Franklin, always with our interests at heart, made a concession to bring grocery boxes on the mail plane for two cents a pound, with a $1.00 minimum. I used to call it the Gravy Plane.

Every household owned a pair of binoculars. They were a handy instrument and we could see all kinds of strange things floating by. One day I said to my young grandson, "Come and take a look at the funny birds riding on a log." The funny birds were Jimmy and Steve, Bill and Linda, jigging out at the reef.

Alice McDonald one time had observed what seemed to be a very large bird on a log with wings outstretched, but she couldn't be sure because of its immobility for such a long period. When she was reasonably sure it was a cormorant, she looked at the clock, then it moved a little, but continued to stand with its wings outstretched. Jimmy Bucknell came up with the answer, that cormorants dive into the water so deep that pressure causes their feathers to become waterlogged, so they just hang them out to dry. They do it for hours on end. I learn something new every day.

Mrs. Mary Chevalier passed away on January 25, 1966. She was 88 years old and was affectionately known as "Ma" or "Gramma Chev." She will be long remembered as a kind and gentle woman, one of the truly greats, belonging to a past era in the San Juan Islands, rich in the pioneering spirit. She was born on Spieden Island where she lived most of her days, maintaining homes on Johns and Stuart Islands. Her husband, Edward A. Chevalier, had preceded her in death in 1958. Their lifetimes here are worthy of a far more gifted and informed pen than this lowly one.

It was a most tempestuous week, a man-against-nature week, with the pilot of the mail plane battling the elements to maintain a steady schedule in the face of 30- to 40-mile-an-hour winds. It was touch and go as he made his scary landings with folks shaking their heads in doubt and then in wonder.

Bob Burn, going down the beach in his weapons carrier to give Roy Bucknell a tow, drove into the water to avoid a log in his path and a three-foot wave washed over him and his vehicle, lifting it up and sucking it in. Using a stump puller, Bob worked feverishly for two hours to keep ahead of an 8-foot incoming tide. Miraculously, the truck still ran after its salt-water bath, but the seats were sure soggy.

Corky North had a few wakeful nights and days of concern for the *Nordland*. With the piles out in the North Bay, he had kept it at the dock on the south side, right in the bight and path of the southeasters and westerlies which had battered our shores of late. Mardi and Corky were toying with the idea of abandoning ship and seeking greener pastures, where there was more life and more opportunity and activity in the school.

I had notions too, but briefly, when I discovered a leak in the roof, a leak in the gas line, a cave-in at my doorstep, and an inconsiderate rat dying in the walls of the basement. As my father would say, anyone who took two sniffs was greedy.

With the freight problem the trend was to go in for miniature packages; I was experimenting with aerosol *Raticate*. I pressed it down on the table top according to instructions and let go. Swoosh! It exploded all over me, and the living room was covered with deadly green whipping cream. If the rain hadn't let up the island may have simply washed away and that would settle all our problems.

Signs of Christmas were beginning to appear at the post office. The traditional Scandinavian knocking bread was hanging by red ribbon, and the Advent calendar and candles were in their second phase. The first Christmas carols were sung around their old grand piano; Salesman Jack returning from his business ventures on the mainland was shaking his head declaring it was terrible, people everywhere were buying like crazy.

Things got a little choppy for the *Blue Fjord*, the Christmas ship from Victoria. I was asked about the children's reaction to their coming; were they excited for weeks, full of anticipation? For way of an answer I told the captain to take a look at their faces—especially the little Carlson girl, she was radiant sitting on Santa's knee, it was pure rapture. I got to sit on Santa's lap too, he had plenty of it and the press has privileges, you know.

Right after Christmas we had a bloomin' blizzard and the snow was a foot deep, more or less, where the wind had blown it and we oldies had some problems. It was tough on the birdies but the children were ecstatic and rosy-cheeked. It was a winter wonderland where the trees have bejeweled branches. I had an occasion to walk out in it with grandson "Bucky" who, wishing to console me for having a wash on the line said, "See, Gramma, it will make the sheets all nice and white." Things had been all nice and white all right, with the roads and snow undisturbed; it was fun identifying all the little markings made by the birds and the bunnies.

There were the footprints of Joe, that was my pet seagull, who used to come up for apples, and then the large indentations were made by "Cinnamon." Jack drove her over to the airstrip just in case the mail plane came in but it was too much for Skyline Air with all that snow and a 20-mile tail wind. We had to hand it to them; it was the first time they had missed, but we were still unhappy about their displacing our boat service.

We missed Corky and Mardi North; their moving to Orcas was not exactly orderly and I could hear her saying, "So we buy sleds for the boys for Christmas and where are the sleds when the snow comes? On Waldron, of course, and where are the boys? On Orcas." They slipped in and out again during the week to pick up the pieces.

We lose a few and we gain a few. The Carlsons were happy to be back in their little trailer house at the logging camp at Park Point. Bill had purchased quite a parcel of land and was logging it. Our gravel supply depot now belonged to Bill but he was very generous with it, and lending a hand with his equipment.

I got the call I was expecting from my sailorman in February direct from the *S.S. Java Mail* via radio telephone, a thousand miles from shore, more marvels of man. I was soon flying high and covering the waterfront. I met Jim in Vancouver, Washington, where we celebrated Thanksgiving and Christmas, and I took a little run down Sound on Grandpa's big ship getting a little dope of life aboard the *Java Mail* and listening to stories of stormy seas and far off lands, of rice, men, and Vietnam.

To a seaman, docking a ship is as common as brushing the teeth but as I watched them docking the *Java Mail* I couldn't help feeling a surge of pride for my mate on the fo'c'sle head as he directed the maneuvering of that huge hulk of steel, bringing it smoothly alongside. The stevedores arrived to run the winches and to stow the cargo of CARE packages, Catholic Welfare bundles, assorted machinery and Bulgar wheat to feed the hungry in India.

With a mind full of plimsoll lines, tonnage, and draft there is not much room for the little woman, but she is here to catch the crumbs and with an armful of shots against tetanus, typhoid, and the plague, there is not much catching up. A little time with the family, cocktails for two with a little candlelight, and it is all over for another four months.

So I headed back to the island, took a few soundings, and got my bearings. Everything had gone off without a hitch when Corky and Mardi came with the *Nordland* landing on Ludwig's beach in a flat calm. The 17,000 feet of lumber for Chuck and Mildred's house was discharged with assembly line precision by their company and many helpers, who seemed to come from every direction. It was a regular beehive; even the littlest girls carried a few boards. I was sure that this house would have a firm foundation and by the look of the joists and mighty beams nothing would be likely to shake it.

The clans had been gathering for Easter. Bob Weaver was back for a spell from his sanitation rounds and planning an addition for Mary's piano. Mary and Chris had been allowed a few days parole from their exile in Neah Bay. Chuck and Mildred were amazed at how the house had grown. And the weeds! If you think I get poetic sometimes you should have heard Bob Burn (master builder) describe the ridge pole he had erected. "It is beautiful, like an arrow pointing into the sun." Doe, Robin, and Mark had come home; Doe still floating on a cloud. Coming back to her beloved island after her isolation from it was a deeply personal thing. She had been teaching pre-school in Seattle and working on another book.

"Be careful what you say, it is the press you are talking to." This is what I would encounter all the time, but the following was one little development I came by freely and without restraint. Marilyn Carlson was so excited, she had just received three packages in the mail; two contained pictures and the other her gold watch and band with a little note from King Size film developers in Everett. She was so taken aback, she didn't know what had become of her watch, she had hunted high and low, how could it have gotten in with her film? The ironic part of it was I told her there was no need to send it first class, never dreaming of the contents. The wonder of it is, how it went through without damage, and the moral could be if you want honest and unusual developments send to King Size.

Took a little gander down to Namu Harbor thinking to see some action at Hollywood and Vine and Lonesome Cove, where they were shooting some scenes for *Namu, The Killer Whale*. It was as deserted as a scene from "High Noon." Maybe it was chow time and everyone was out to lunch. Nobody discovered me even though I sang a few chanties with the boys. I was reminded that it was not that kind of sea story and they had all the local color they needed. You can't blame a gal for trying.

Phil Lovering never ceased to amaze me. A couple of years back he imported a plantation, setting it in the middle of the forest, and recruiting Bob Burn and others to develop an elaborate water system and to work on plans for a house, complete with library and conservatory. Last summer he was traveling in Europe and Bob Burn received a letter from him saying, "Hold everything, I have a new plan for a Swiss chalet." We were looking forward to his retirement in the fall and now he had written us that there was no urgency on the construction. Instead of retiring he had taken another job as head of the bridge design department of Singstod and Kehart, New York engineering firm. Next thing he would be writing us that he had taken a bride; nothing would have surprised us at that point.

Things were in a very bad state of affairs; the pigeons had brought up reinforcements and it was a race between them and the caterpillars, which of them would destroy the cherry trees first. The caterpillars were creeping and chewing, they were in the house and in the car, they were in the soup and in my hair. I understand that they have a natural enemy; those little white spots on their heads are the eggs of the ignumen fly which finally destroys them, but that year there may have not been enough flies to go around; there were trillions of caterpillars.

Then there were the starlings that rob nests and fight off all the little birds at the feeders. Mac thought he had a cure for that, a pull of the trigger and pow! pow! The rest of the flock flew over in formation, looked down at their departed brother and never returned. The year before, Margaret Severson thought she had hit upon just the thing and ordered a plastic owl. Now, those little cherry blossom stem cutters took one look at it and fled while others went right on pecking away and were so bold as to perch right on the owl's head. I, too, thought I had discovered a panacea for all bird problems, a bird barrier with claims so diversified that I had filled out the coupon immediately with the taste of juicy red cherries already in my mouth. It was a rope of acrylic mesh which you simply lifted over your trees or spread over your strawberries. It was so soft and silky, something one could imagine belonging to the boudoir rather than a bird deterrent. I was crestfallen but not beaten. I was bound to have my pound of cherries in spite of all the head shaking. I recruited some help, but had not counted on the wind. Everyone got hopelessly entangled and the wind carried it away to an old snag and there it hung like one enormous caterpillar tent. We were such purists, if we were ever caught spraying we would have been excommunicated from the inner circle. I didn't know; it was a temptation and I was weakening.

Lizanne Magraw had been the school teacher for seven years; now she was resigning and in the jolly month of June the community gathered once again to observe one of Lizanne's charming little dramas and to hear the little students of piano. Mike, Melanie, Martha, and Lisa played their pieces by Bach and an assortment of familiar melodies. Chairman of the Board, Bob Burn, presented a diploma to our one eighth-grade graduate, Kristi Magraw, with simple but packed-with-meaning and straight-from-the-heart words of congratulation. As Clerk of the Board, I felt I had failed miserably as a speech maker, for as I practically thrust the departing gift from the community at Lizanne, words failed me. She had been the backbone of the school, giving so much and asking so little. Lizanne had contributed five bright little girls to the cause of giving added weightings to pupil enrollment (perhaps this last may be over your head, but it was the latest allotment jargon). Lizanne went on to perpetuate her education at graduate school at the University of Washington.

On June 10th there was another simple ceremony enacted, possibly the first of its kind—a beach wedding. In keeping with their Mennonite background of simplicity, Mary and Bob Weaver dispensed with all the fuss and ado of a church wedding when their daughter, Josie, and Tony Scruton plighted their troth. Their altar was of driftwood, and the music, the sound of the surf and sea birds calling. The marriage feast was a good old salmon barbecue with suitable side dishes. It was strictly a family affair with the groom's father, the Reverend Norman Scruton, officiating. The Reverend and Mrs. Scruton were from Forks, Washington. The happy couple bided a wee on Waldron.

Jim had been sailing on the *Java Mail* for over a year and supposedly had earned a 70-day vacation, but owing to the *emergency* he was only allowed a week. Heretofore he would spend his precious days at home working on the house or caulking, scraping, and painting the *Fifty-Fifty*. I felt that he deserved better than that, so, for Father's Day, we, Fran, and the family, planned a surprise for him with a new 18-foot "Pacific Mariner" cabin job which we named the *Java Jim*. So Jim spent his precious days in the San Juans running his new baby, transporting the grandkids to and from Friday Harbor. His next assignment was skipper of the *Red Oak Victory* sailing to the Far East.

Fran's breadwinner, Billy, returned from Bristol Bay and reported a fair season salmon-wise, but the weather was rough with continual rain and winds up to 70- and 80-miles-per, in which a dozen people had lost their lives and boats, floundering on sandbanks with no possible means of rescue.

Bill's gillnetter, which he keeps in Alaska, is named the *St. Elmo*, after the patron saint of sailors. Many people have seen St. Elmo's fire, a strange electrical phenomenon. I remember my father telling of seeing it in the rigging of sailing ships, and my sailorman had also seen it in the form of a ball sitting on the mast and gradually fading away into nothingness. Mardi and Corky North had a group of 30 people in to watch the Seafair races on TV. It was in midsummer and when a sudden downpour of rain came, St. Elmo got in the race with his ball dancing along the porch rail, adding extra excitement to the affair.

Over and over we were reminded of how fortunate we were to have the service of Island Sky Ferries and how literally the term "Life line of the islands" could be applied. We had expressed our deep gratitude to Roy Franklin for caring for us, for the feeling of trust he inspired. In the business world he may never be among the greats, but if gratitude and admiration count for anything, he is indeed a rich man. A little bouquet was in order for Irving French, too, who sensed something was amiss when he saw the commotion on North Bay shore and warmed up his battery operated transmitter in case there was an emergency. When he learned that a young boy was adrift in the tide on his overturned kayak, he called Island Sky and in a matter of minutes Roy was on the scene.

The water had been sparkling blue, calm and inviting when the two boys, Ramsey Embick and Terrigal Burn, had taken off in high boyish spirits across the channel in their kayaks, but they had not known of the danger of the swift currents and flooding tide rips, and Ramsey's craft capsized in the churning waters. Ramsey was only 14, but a champion swimmer, and he had the presence of mind to stay with the kayak while Terrigal paddled ashore for help. A search by speedboat and passing cruisers was unsuccessful, but eagle-eyed Roy spotted him from his seaplane and picked him up in the open water two-thirds of the way to Pender Island where the tide had carried him. All up and down the beach people wept. Tragedy was averted, the boys learned a valuable lesson, and once again Roy Franklin was our hero.

Chapter Eighteen
Cross Currents
1966-1967

With the Magraw family preparing to leave the island, Lizanne, as a parting gesture, wanted once again to hear some of the old records which recalled so many memories. So, after several years of inertia we rustled up a dance and the old log cabin wall resounded with music. It was an impromptu affair with soft candlelight and firelight inside, and Cynthia's beam shining over the waters, outside.

Rolf Thorson, with his mechanical know-how, fixed the old record player and battery loud speaker and the music went around and around. The teenagers seemed to have a monopoly on the music box. They called it modern but it looked pretty primitive to me. All those gyrations and gestures looked like a primitive rain dance that could provoke the gods to most anything. Couldn't exactly say it was like old times, but we managed to squeeze in the *Tennessee Waltz* for Ralph Wood, *Hernando's Hideaway*, and *O, My Papa* and you should have seen us oldies make a dash for the floor. Oh, what fun, and what memories, a time when we had inspired such names as Lady, Duchess, or Countess, according to one's style and deportment on the floor. All that I could evoke was, "Oh, you're just a pleasant peasant."

Josie and Tony, our honeymoon couple, had returned from their canoe trip and their family was growing by leaps and bounds. They had found it hard to keep the wolf from the door. (Couldn't resist that one.) Their wolf pup, Lupi gave Mary an amorous nip on the nose. Contrary to belief, wolves are not vicious by nature and they must by taught to hunt by the mother. Lupi loved anything made of leather and was very sensitive; when he was chided he turned on that soulful look. The question was how would they ever go about getting him off the island.

In the fall of 1966, we were proud to add to our list of notables in the news. Our own Waldron author, Doris Burn, was presented with a gold medal, the Pacific Northwest Seller's Award for the best juvenile book of the year, *Andrew Henry's Meadow*. She had the further distinction of having the highest sales for juvenile literature in the state of Washington. Her book had gone over so well in the United States that the first edition was now being published in England. To those who knew Bob Burn, it came as quite a surprise when he decided to make a trip to see his folks, June and Farrar, in Marianna, Florida. He was the boy who said he would never, no never, leave the island again, but he had worked up quite an enthusiasm for it and was as excited as a kid when he left. He went by train so he would miss the billboards; he didn't want anything to do with jets. Bob was the original poor country boy, his riches were in the gold in the morning sun, etc. On his return, our smiling wayfarer, after being plied with questions, said that he was force-fed like a Strasbourg goose, including the pâté de foie gras.

The island had a tranquilizing effect on my sister, Marian, living in a dream world as opposed to the jingle, jangle of the city, and the unobstructed view, after the wall to wall chimney pots. She went on her way again with her bags full of driftwood and shells. The beaches were well gleaned of agates after all the summer hunters, but she had enjoyed her trips in the *Java Jim*, even the very last one which had worried her so when the wind and tide took us onto the rocks and Jim had to untangle my fishing gear from the wheel of the outboard. The wheel got somewhat bent when Jim said, "Amidships," and I put it, "Full ahead." After Marian had climbed the ladder to the dock, she stooped down with a sigh to kiss the deck, she was so glad to be on dry land again.

As Halloween approached I was reading up on some

ghost stories, getting into the spirits of the times. It was in the good old days in Don Chaotic's time of masquerades, Mardi Gras, and the pranks they had played. Someone had substituted ether in his hookah and he was having hallucinations of riding in a blue tunnel in his rickshaw with a crowd of children chasing him, of rescuing a beautiful harem girl, and just as she was about to bestow a kiss of gratitude upon his lips he had been aroused by his mate saying it was time to catch his plane. There was a lady in black who had really crashed the party when she tripped over the lantern at the door; the absent-minded professor came in his underwear and a black tie. Crazy Neighbor had tried to affect a Gandhi drape but settled for an Arab because he couldn't find a Bedouin. We used to have a devil of a time, all on a little spiced cider. Ah, me! All the dear departed spirits.

It wasn't a pipe dream that Marjorie French was having when she beach-combed a 50-pound sack of flour. Cammy Burn had also found a sack of flour which had lost its way, it was stamped "CARE" for delivery to India. A third recipient didn't know whether to be glad or mad for she had just sent a contribution to the cause. Now Jim had a watertight explanation for it, but maybe the moral of the incident could be, "Cast thy bread upon the waters and it will return to you in a soggy sack."

The island was about at its lowest ebb, some 30 souls, but at Thanksgiving it was spilling over again. It held special significance for Chuck and Mildred Ludwig, who celebrated their first dinner party in their lofty new log cabin castle. Needless to say, I was a very happy lady with Jim home for the occasion after many moons at sea, and with my little family of boat enthusiasts all together. Bill and Lizzie came over from Friday Harbor in the *Flumpy*, a name which the grandkids had lovingly bestowed on Grandpa Bill and his boat. They made their way in a dense fog without the aid of a compass, just using their "water wisdom." Weather didn't seem to daunt this little sea-faring family. When they took off in the *Sharon Linda* I could just hear that little voice say, "Gee, Mama, it's a little wavy," as the water rushed by the portholes. This was Mitchell at three years old.

As the old year was coming to a close, sadness and grief came to our dwindling little community when our friend and neighbor, Emory Johnson, passed away at his home here. He had a momentary pain, lay back his head, and that was the end of his 75 useful years. Emory was a hardworking, fun loving, and swarthy man, born in Sweden in 1891, and coming to the U.S.A. in 1907. His life story had been intermingled with the history of Waldron since his marriage to Elvida Dahlbeck, and bits and pieces of their lives together are strewn among the pages of this story.

Now to pick up a few threads of life with Captain Jim, who in the year of 1967 was standing by his latest ship, the *Bowdoin Victory*, which was in dry dock being readied for sea duty. I joined him in San Diego, and, for an old lotus-eater, I did some swift and lofty living. The jet age—it's mad, it's moving, and mighty handy; a far cry from our lowly little island pace. Roy Bucknell was my leave replacement at the post office, dishing out the stamps and reading the postcards. Roy was very efficient but didn't like publicity; nevertheless, we were very much aware of his presence in the community and the kindly little things he did in his own quiet way.

I was kept informed by mail as Roy wrote, "All's great here, quiet and tranquil, no riots, no protest marches, crime rate down to zero, very light traffic patterns." (Quite often we could track down a neighbor to tell who had been where by their car tracks.)

Mary Weaver wrote, "Bright sunshine here, birds singing madly and already establishing their territories, troops of robins in the fields and lawn, looking for worms and scolding each other." Sounded like spring with all that bird talk, and no doubt the snowdrops were blooming down Hawthorn Lane. There was a 90-mile-an-hour wind which had damaged the *Nordland* when it slammed against the dock; the uprights were dashed off, and the ramp cut loose. The school went on apace with all four lads progressing and a minimum of absenteeism.

Meanwhile down south, Jim and I were taking in the sights across the border, and dog races, jai alai games, and a glass-blowing shop. We visited the famous zoo, the old missions, and Ramona marriage house. There isn't much left of the old way of life and countryside since the advent of the bulldozer, which makes room to accommodate those who come to see the lovely orange groves. Progress and expansion—where will it end and what will there be left to see?

We said our goodbyes again when Jim and his ship pulled away from the dock in San Diego for sea trials, loaded cargo at Long Beach, then off to the land of troubled waters.

I was soon back behind bars, in the post office, that is. It was only a figure of speech, no bars here of any kind. In my absence, County Agent Joe Long had been over visiting the school and discussing fruits and small berries and conferring with Corky and Mardi about importing some new blood for their livestock. Shortly after, he made another visit, bringing his pot of wax, an assortment of wicked looking saws and knives, and a mind full of know-how, which he eagerly and interestingly imparted to others. It was Waldron's turn to have a grafting demonstration, so the school children and a few onlookers hovered around one of George Lindsey's old apple trees to watch Joe perform some magic with scions and bud sticks, and making the several types of grafts; whips, cleft, bark, and side. One individual, genuinely seeking knowledge of this amazing art, wanted to know who was the discoverer of the process, thinking it might be Luther Burbank or one of the great horticulturists of the century. She learned it had been going on for thousands of years. We had anticipated some strange developments, maybe some cherries growing on the apple tree.

These experiments at Baer's Lair and Juniper Cove Ranch were successful and Corky got that old back-to-the-land urge and was revitalizing and replenishing the old impoverished orchard of Ethan Allen days. Mardi visited Marble's lath house in Friday Harbor and came back loaded with plants. She was down on her knees staging a dig-in with lots of help from little Terry. Mardi had quite the flair for landscaping but her defenses were rather poor; those strumpet cows walked all over her mini-waterfall.

The distant rumblings and fear of change to our island life style brought us together at the Weaver's for a follow-up meeting and the next stop in planning a poll of what the community wanted for its future. Dr. Bill Cook presided and, as in all such groups, there was a division of thought. There were those who would like to keep the island as primitive as possible; two rooms and a path, water from the well, kerosene lamps, and the like. Others wished for a little more ease and comfort in living, especially the older folks. Some would like more young families with children to perpetuate the school. We were concerned about roads, the upkeep of the dock and the airfield, sanitation and good water, which would all be threatened as the summer population increased. Some would like to keep the island as a bird sanctuary; several people had seen two wild swans in the swamp. At first they had looked like a boat, but with glasses it showed the male with a female dutifully following in his wake. At McDonald's it was a regular aviary. There were plenty of feeders and enticements and birds of all colors and breeds free to feed and fly together unafraid.

Happiness is an island in the sun. Happiness is going barefoot in the sand. Happiness is digging a clam and prying an oyster, finding an agate and watching the sandpipers at the edge of the sea. Happiness is making a garden, eating your first radishes and seeing a dogwood in bloom, kids playing baseball, and having the lawn mower start right off. Fran and Bill had been up in the *Sharon Linda* improving the shining hours around their place, and said happiness is when they get the children to bed after a day of hard playing, bruises, scratches, and falling overboard. Lizzie was the envy of the aggregate agate collectors, having found a beautiful agate arrowhead in her garden patch.

The next time I was storming Seattle with my mate, Tony Scruton gave us all a nice surprise by writing the Waldron Word in my absence. Nothing like a shot of new blood, and nice for me to be on the receiving end for a change. As he had written, here are a few island tidbits for the curiosity seekers.

Trucks, jeeps, and similar inventions of the devil have of late been the object of long hours of frustration and a peppering of unsightly language. Roy Bucknell's jeep developed arthritis in the front end and left him traveling by shank's mare for awhile, but a few vitamins and spare parts renewed its vigor. On the other hand, Mac (pen name of N.C. McDonald), seems to prefer all his troubles at once. He managed to get two flats and a bum rear wheel in the same day, which had made him rather unapproachable for awhile. To make things even frostier, he sent the tires to town and then discovered he had shipped off one of the good tires and still had a flat on his hands. The joys of living on an island are sometimes not too obvious.

Tony Scruton amazed the local populace by fixing his truck that has been out of commission for many months. It took a couple of days to repair it, since he had a hard time fitting such things into his busy schedule. If he doesn't do something about those rusty floor boards, he'll find himself peddling the truck from the ground one of these days. Someday we'll all go to heaven where there won't be any gasoline engines.

Noisy neighbor, Bob Burn, developed a bum knee while maneuvering through his work area so decided to go to Seattle to see his kids; however, Mark and Robin decided to come to the island to see him, so his weekend mission was not entirely successful. He did have a delicious-sounding Chinese dinner with Doe, Cameron, and Lisa, and those things are a little hard to come by on Waldron. But, then Seattle doesn't have red-winged blackbirds in the middle of

October and that is what Margaret Severson has. It must mean we're going to have a hard winter, or maybe a mild one—or maybe no winter at all. Since the advent of the weatherman, the birds don't have much control over things any more.

If you see someone go by in a black leather jacket and helmet on his motorcycle, think nothing of it. It is probably Irving French on his new motorcycle. But then you better make sure as you can never tell who's on the island nowadays.

The local timber wolf has taken to sleeping under the Scruton's dinner table. There are certain risks in this since he doesn't like anyone to put their feet under the table and it's tough eating supper three feet from the table. Trouble is, when he stands up he carries the table off with him! All kinds of hazards in this island living.

* * *

I left Jim in fine fettle and ready again to pilot the *Bowdoin Victory* and her crew into foreign waters and to tackle the typhoons. We were then communicating by tape recorder, a one-sided affair but quite an invention.

I asked around if anything new and exciting had happened in my absence. The reply was lukewarm. It had been raining too much and spirits were low. Well, there's excitement in each new day, watching the wind and the waves dashing on the shore. Suddenly it would clear and everything would be bathed in sunlight. I can even get excited about seaweed which the sea so conveniently sets up on the beach, and if you ever doubt its potency as a fertilizer you should have seen the Weaver's Sweetmeat squash; fourteen of them from two vines and each averaging 35 to 40 inches in diameter. These are considered to be a small squash; wonder what it would do to a Hubbard?

Ruth Little, Jack Magraw's cousin, who dedicated her time and energies to helping disturbed children, would find relaxation on her visits to the island. However, this one time on a cold November night she felt that the island had been a little unfriendly, not people-wise, of course, but small wonder with rats running about; she had encountered one in the kitchen, not looking very lively. Someone told her that when a rat was sick it wasn't afraid of people, so Ruth huddled unhappily in front of the fireplace, expecting any moment to be attacked. Then Cinnamon, that was the horse, had her buffaloed; it had found a loophole in the fence and her attempt to coax it back into the corral with apples had been of no avail. Then she had thought of oats, but she couldn't find any, but came upon a sack which had the appearance of grain and that turned the trick. Later she almost panicked when she remembered the 50-pound sack of rat poison which Jack had brought up and wondered if this was what she had fed the horse! Should she try to make it to the Frenches and call the vet over the citizen's band? It was a pitch black night and the wind was howling, so she abandoned the idea and spent the long night in fear and doubt. In the morning she gathered up some of the contents of the sack that she had used and hied herself over to the McDonald's, who calmed her fears with a quick analysis. Ruth had not poisoned the horse after all, it was just plain grain.

I had been toying with the idea of resigning as island reporter, but after all the nice words of welcome home I felt I should at least acknowledge them. I had been feeling rather inferior in the interior while I was down South with Jim; the doctor suggested I go to the hospital and have some tests made. It took a little getting used to the lazy, hazy days in San Francisco, nothing to do but eat and sleep and read. I was beginning to like the idea until someone sent me a sprig of balm of Gilead (pretty sneaky); it jolted me right out of my lethargy. Acacia trees weren't so bad but when the balm began to waft through my hospital room, I had some explaining to do. Strange no one had heard of the San Juan Islands, but they did when I was through and most of the hospital staff and some of the inmates were going to move up there en masse.

There really hadn't been much wrong with me, nothing but what a little jogging could help. I was thinking of joining the great fraternity of runners; it was the latest fad to keep you fit. If you couldn't run a mile in 12 minutes, then you were considered a creep-er. Later I learned that ten minutes of skipping was worth thirty of jogging.

I hied me home on the next plane and a double rainbow arching over Skipjack Island greeted me. There were diamonds on the white birches when the sun shone through the rain like hundreds of shimmering prisms. There was winter blooming jasmine up at Phil's place and morel mushrooms popping up; Margaret Severson had cut fresh daffodils and violets in February and sent them airmail to her daughter-in-law, Ab's wife, Eunice, in Alaska. Both of Margaret's sons were then working for the Alaska Ferries.

Another sure sign of the times—when folks would abandon the warmth of the old iron stove and move out to the post office steps into the morning sun, where all the important issues of the island were hashed out. Who would be our next postmaster? Would there be any children for the school in the fall? Who would make the first move to have a work bee on the dock? Was it safe to plant your peas yet, and how could we get rid of wire worms without poison?

The invaders were back, the *Malacasoma Americano*, spawn of the Lepidoptera, were causing a caterpillar catastrophe, the hairy hordes were attacking the roses and the raspberries, creeping, crawling, chewing and sucking after denuding the cherry and apple trees, leaving them shrouded in an eerie web. It was indeed a sorry situation.

The Captain came home on vacation at last and it was 0600, four bells and all's well; never did quite get the hang of this nautical time telling and shipboard jargon. The kitchen was a galley, the stove pipe a Charley Noble, and the dining room a mess. Jim said that seafaring was never like this; kindling fires and stirring up his wife's breakfast while she stares at the typewriter keys wondering what has been going on all week.

I had been singing the praises of Waldron for so many

years I thought there was nothing new under the sun; I had said it all. Then some wonderful person spurs me on, my patient husband who puts up with my Monday morning moods, and friends returning from the cities, bright-eyed and full of the wonder of it all; newcomers discovering the sights and sounds and smells for the first time, and always my grateful readers.

Had an inquiry awhile back about what had become of Waldron's wolf, the four-legged one owned by the Scrutons. I was under sort of a gentleman's agreement not to divulge its whereabouts. Now it could be told. It had been on Flattop Island where Tony and Josie were camping and where Lupi was able to expend his exuberance without incident and be free of the fetters of society. He was not a gentle soul and his greeting bowled one over.

I came upon a little scene on the Sand Flats one day. Lupi and Trash, the red setter, were taking Tony for a run when they met Peppy, the Chevalier's toy fox terrier, who was all bristling, ready to take on the pair. His bark was the voice of inexperience and his innocence would not have been bliss if he became too bold. Lupi had grown at least six feet tall on his hind feet. He was licking Billy's ear while making friends with the Chevalier children.

Lupi loved the water and swam all the way from Flattop to Waldron, a distance of three miles, without the least sign of exhaustion. He was a beautiful animal, but Tony realized that they had a problem, especially with more and more people coming to the island who did not know of the wolf's personal history.

The Chevalier beach looked like a bit of Coney Island with all the people here. The Nashes and the Guards; the Carlsons and their cousins and their cousins' cousins; the *Sharon Linda* and the *St. James* were there; row boats and speedy boats, a hydroplane and surfriders.

Our grandson, Matty Boy, had come up with an idea to solve the school problem by saying, "Why not have the school in the summer-times? Lots of kids on the island then." Matty Boy's nautical heritage was cropping up early and he knew all the words to the song, "What shall we do with the drunken Sailor." He sang it at kindergarten and almost shocked his teacher when he sang the last verse, "Shave his belly with a rusty razor."

Bob and Betty Graber, too, had been discovering the feel and essence of the island with a few pointers from June Burn's book, *Living High*, sampling sea lettuce and catching all kinds of strange denizens of the deep. They tackled a 40-pound ling cod. (Incidentally, I read that a ling is not a cod, but some kind of turbot. It sure had me fooled all these years) They weren't quite sure what to so with it. Betty fled into the cabin when it started to thrash around (they hadn't heard of a gaff hook yet) so they towed it ashore. I asked her how they killed it, "Oh," she said, "we just drowned it." The next unidentified fish that they hooked onto they clobbered with the flag staff. Well, it takes all kinds.

The tragedy of the plane crash in which pilot Tom Sedlicas and Ivan Brower of Friday Harbor lost their lives was felt by everyone on Waldron. We had the deepest sympathy for their families and for Roy Franklin who had to bear the heart-heavy burden for the loss of a fine pilot and the plane he was flying, and for the interruption of the long years of accident-free operation of Island Sky Ferries, which had become so much a part of the island life. This tragedy had affected even the very young and it was eight-year-old Matthew again, who said to me as he helped to raise the flag at the post office, "Gramma, shouldn't it be at half mast; you know, the flyers who died?" "Yes, dear, I know, but that is only for very important people, like presidents, etc." "But, Gramma," he said, "pilots are important people." Yes, yes, how true, and how strange are the ways of fate.

Chapter Nineteen
Ebbing Tides
1968-1970

When the summer folk left there was a hush in the air, and when the drifting morning mists lifted, it would be another Indian summer, like standing still in time when one could take a breath, catch up, and dwell on all the fun times we had with our kin and friends.

There was now only a handful of us left to sit in the sunshine on the post office steps while waiting for the mail. Joe Long, the County Agent, had taken time out from his busy schedule to pay Waldron a visit. He was about to retire. He sat with us awhile and talked of earthquakes, when islands had been known to simply disappear (comforting thought). He inspected some of Phil's plantings and advised some pruning; discovered oak root rot fungus and gall on my rose bushes and advised me.

Phil was here from New York enjoying our cool weather and living in a world of house plans. He would only deviate from his elevations and draftsman's board for a jaunt in the *Java Jim*, and to confer with Roy Bucknell, keeper of the trees and grounds, Bob Burn, his master builder, and Bob Weaver, well and septic tank expert.

No sound of the old school bell that year, no little people peeping and waving from the windows as we passed by on our way to the airfield. Such a pity, but I suppose people need people and children need playmates and teachers need stimulation. Mary Weaver would be getting hers fishing on the waters and gathering mushrooms in the woods and playing on her piano and a little catching up with her son, Andy, who was gone for over a year to New York pursuing his favorite pastime, the opera.

Marilyn Carlson once said she was going to write a

book and call it *Crisis Island*; she seemed to be facing one most of the time. When Bill Carlson went out the front door, trouble came in the back. The family had just returned from Disneyland and were not exactly ready for the rigors of island life in an unfurnished A-frame in the face of all the elements. It was a far cry from the placid waters of summer and the gentle sunrises over Mount Baker, so Marilyn was quite unnerved when Bill failed to return from Orcas, but then no one was able to return to Waldron in such a howling wind and the highest tide known around here for fifteen years.

Mrs. Elizabeth Chevalier, known affectionately as Lizzie or by her grandchildren as Gramma Sugar (she was a diabetic), and Gramma Wizzie by the wee ones, passed away on September 25, 1968. To Waldron it meant not only the loss of a friend, but one of the few remaining Waldron pioneers.

Lizzie had not great riches except the land she was raised upon, but she left a legacy rich in island lore which I have sprinkled here and there throughout these pages. She learned at a very early age to take the responsibilities of a household, her mother having a very painful eye affliction which had ended in blindness. At the age of eleven she took on the care of a motherless baby whom she called Girlie and raised her as one of the family.

Lizzie's life had been a full one, but not an easy one. She faced the inevitable, as she faced life, with a forthrightness; whatever had to be done, she did it; what was to be, she accepted it with grace. She was dedicated to the old fashioned principles of good family relations, a staunch, down-to-earth mother and grandmother. If Mrs. Chevalier had a message to leave her many children it would simply be: "Now be good kids and mind your parents."

Bob and Mary Weaver took a trip back to Indiana where they had interests in the seedless watermelon business. It was Mary's first trip home since coming here ten years before. In the meantime, we were pelted with hailstones; our lovely golden leaves lay sodden by the roadside, ready to be scooped up for the compost; nothing is ever wasted in nature.

Days were getting shorter and Halloween came and went without incident; no motley crowd tripping to the schoolhouse; no cats or bats or goblins; no witches' brew or magical music; no dancing, prancing, or little people; just ghosts, ghosts, ghosts and a big moon shining down on the silence. Then it was November, a month of many facets and surprises; when the sun breaks through the leaden shrouds, behold! the majesty of the snowcapped Olympics bathed in feathery loveliness. Soon there was frost on the dock and a nice new shake roof on the shed, Bob Burn thought shakes were more befittin' than composition.

The winter of 1968-1969 was a winter not soon to be forgotten with some new stories to tell the grandchildren which might top the old timers' tales. We would remember how Mr. Northeast Wind, Esquire, blew his icy breath across the water, whipping up a topping of misty peaks which reached up to meet the clouds while temperatures went zooming down to zero; how the snow fell and stayed, and froze, thawed and froze again, making for bad roads and airfields; how planes were grounded and larders ran low; the pipes and pumps which froze and power that failed. I could just hear my father declaring another ice age.

We heard it from all around, the bad side and the sad side and yet it had its glad side; the aesthetic beauty of the snow softly falling, blanketing the countryside with its purity, and the sledding and skating, happy and rosy cheeked youngsters, chopping ice and melting snow when faucets refused to function.

Snow water is so soft and makes very good coffee; you may get a fir needle or a little Madrona bark now and then, but that would give the tea a zesty flavor. Did you know that it takes two pails of packed snow to make two quarts of water? A little time-consuming if you were contemplating a bath, but it has its merits.

I was thrice thwarted in my attempt to meet Jim in San Francisco, but that was all water under the bridge and my problems were peanuts compared to the Captain's as he piloted his ship across the Pacific, battling winds up to 70 miles an hour and 32-foot seas which at times had the ship rolling to a 40-degree angle, all seven thousand tons of it. The *Bowdoin Victory* was then resting in temporary lay-up and Jim was back at the helm on the hill.

Three cheers for Corky North who braved our blizzard to bring us much needed supplies and freight. Corky bought out the lumber and supply business from George Gow at Eastsound and this was to be his last trip with the ferry *Nordland*, having sold it to Bob Greenway of Deer Harbor.

The ice finally broke up, the herring boats were back in the bay, and folks were all smiles again and the birds began to sing the day the wind shifted to the southeast. The snow may have been driven, but it was pure no more. I think it is safe to say it was the worst winter since 1906. Waldron didn't fare so badly, though; our kerosene and butane lamps served us well with no power cables to worry about. We had water from various sources and plenty of wood to burn. The Island Mail, Inc., made courageous efforts to keep the mail and groceries coming and occasional callers to and fro.

Interesting hidden talents and occupations sprang up to stave off cabin fever. Barometer tapping became a daily pastime and making home-made ice cream was not so bad. Tony Scruton said the skating was superb; so did Bob Weaver before he got all bruised up, when the ice gave way.

They always came when you least expected them and it was one of those piercingly cold days that the Post Office Inspector arrived. We must have presented a motley picture, folks all bundled up to the eyebrows in scarves and hoods and shod in mukluks and boots while he, in contrast, wore the conventional businessman's attire without the benefit of hat or long johns. He seemed comforted to back up to the old iron stove; there's nothing like it to warm that which needs to be warmed.

As we meandered into March our hiemal visitations were retreating into the past and our thoughts to the murmuring of spring. Gene and Helen Hill, trusting souls as they were, came up from Tacoma to plant their peas and potatoes on the conventional date, George Washington's birthday.

So goes the Waldron world, no big scoops, just little gleanings and happenstances from a rural routine, like the time the water finally thawed out and Jim and I gazed at it trickling from the faucet and with a happy squeal embraced each other as though we had struck oil.

Fred McNaught was asking, "Where have all the birdies gone?" He hadn't seen any since the cold spell, but then his range of vision was rather limited, being confined to his wheelchair with only a small windowpane through which to watch the cars go by and tell the direction of the wind by the swaying of the trees. Of course, the rest of us knew that the birds were all over at the McDonald's; they knew on which side their bread was buttered. Juncos, towhees, rosy finches and the song sparrows, Alaska robins and maybe a falcon, peregrine, or kestrel; you name 'em, they have 'em. I was playing nursemaid to a bunch of dive bombers, a simple syrup slave to a flock of ruddy Rufuses, but they were so fascinating. A little bird told me that hummingbirds fly all the way to South America to spend the winter, and to think that they have the instinct and the same feeders. In fact, it's amazing.

Oh, for the life on the bounding main and a little more full speed, captain, please. Jim was pacing the deck again, had enough landlubbering, so he was steaming full ahead to San Francisco again to join his ship, the *Mayfield Victory*. Ironically all his seabags and gear had been shipped to the island; now it all had to go back, fair weather and foul gear, cold weather and tropical gear, navigation books, sextant, tape recorder, and radio. Sailors have to have gobs of gear and San Juan Airlines could hardly get off the ground when the Captain was aboard. So now that gallant guy in the galley was gone and I had to burn my own Monday morning toast for a spell.

One fine day in May, Postmaster Charles Nash of Friday Harbor made a trip this way bringing Postal Services Officer Lyle Simons of Everett to visit the post office here, and to meet its master (technically there is no such thing as a postmistress) and to get a better understanding of any problems (if we had any) and be of service to us. Mr. Simons seemed to be fascinated by the quiet, roomy log building and backwoods furnishings, gas light, and oxen yoke overhead, a relic of old times when Waldron was ploughed and deforested with oxen.

There were no patrons at the time. I'm afraid they were still mad at the department for taking to the air, thus depriving the island of freight and passenger service; not that we had any complaints with Island Mail, it was just a way of life that was suitable for the island.

We had to face it, this was the jet age with fast transportation and it brought great opportunities for our young people to travel abroad, but it was always nice to have the island to come back to.

Joe Goodrich, who had been with the Peace Corps for two years, got a hearty welcome back. He was about to embark on another adventure, which in Joe's own words he thought would blow his mind. He was a member of an expedition, and they were going to hunt and recover lost treasures from old sunken Spanish galleons off the coast of Honduras.

Joe was highly enthusiastic and it sounded like something out of a storybook, but they were supposed to have documented proof that the gold was there. The expedition didn't turn out as expected though, and we didn't get the pistoles and doubloons he promised to bring us.

"It's pink! It's a girl!" All eyes went heavenward as the

tender toilet tissue slowly unfurled from its roll in the sky. Trust Roy Franklin to enter into the spirit of the island's little blessed event with feeling and gentle humor, buzzing over the housetop bringing the news to Mary Weaver that she was a grandmother. On June 24, 1969, a baby girl was born to Josie and Tony Scruton in Anacortes. They named her Sophie and she was the first island baby we had had since Martha Magraw, some ten years back.

Elaine Cook had said to me, "What we need in these troubled times is to cherish more of the old ideals and honor our forebears." Martha Magraw, one young modern who had not yet left the fold, cajoled her mother into reviving the old island custom of a Fourth of July picnic; at least the art of eating together was still in vogue. So up went the smoke signals and the drums rumbled and all roads led to the familiar picnic grounds as some of the gang assembled their potluck pots.

Russ Thorson said this good old-fashioned laugh-in revived his soul; no matter how far and wide they travel, Waldron will always be home to Russ and the boys. Rolf, who had been serving in the Peace Corps in India, returned for a visit. Leaving as a boy, Rolf had returned as a man of experience with several inches added to his stature.

OO! Ouch! Leggo! I almost got lost in the forest last night as I made my way through the dense undergrowth with Queen Mab and four little woodland nymphs who tripped merrily through the briars with their little buckets, dodging the 'skeeters, the nettles and thistles, and over tinder-dry brush and fallen logs. The berries were hard to come by now, with so many people finding our favorite patches. Blackberry vines have a way of changing their spots, they need stirring up and a nice new pile of brush to trail over; that is where the loggers come in handy. Logging on Waldron had long been a controversial topic with some taking a dim view of it. Logging had left ugly scars, but nature can get rather untidy herself when left to her own devices; little seedlings need space to breathe. Many times loggers had conveniently opened up and given access to a wood supply to those who had no woodland of their own.

Bob Hartzog, editor and owner of the *Friday Harbor Journal*, passed away in August, 1969. I really only knew him in connection with the *Journal* as a correspondent during my fleeting office visits. At such times he treated me with friendliness and quick wit. I will always be grateful to Bob and Mildred for printing the "Waldron Word," which, had it not been for the *Journal*, may have been lost to posterity.

During the winter of 1968, when the town had been in darkness and without power after a cable had broken, there was a time when Bob wondered if his efforts to run the paper were worthwhile. And then it hit. Bill Mason drew the cleverest cartoon depicting the *Journal* office, as Bob, with a questioning countenance, was warming his hands and derriere by an old black iron heater, Mildred in her visor sat at the linotype machine setting up the type. The caption read, "Live Better Electrically."

This brought a response from people and friends from all over the globe; it made a great impression. Mildred wrote to me, "Bob walks with his back a little straighter now."

Tommy and Jean Thomas were next to take charge of our little weekly and it was to them I now offered my humble scribblings.

It was a beautiful morning, waters a little ruffled, barometer falling, the mate sleeping on his watch, communication poor, wind straight up and down, and I was off course with the log not up-to-date. In other words, I had overslept and I had to hustle to catch the *Bronco* express. We were living in two different worlds; the pressures of war and responsibilities of mastering a vessel were beginning to take their toll.

On Jim's last voyage to Vietnam an attempt was made to blow up the ship. Two unobtrusive-looking characters in a sampan, full of dynamite, had been caught paddling around the stern of the ship while in port.

Jim had been warned, because of a heart condition, to take it easy. We made our first step toward retirement by purchasing a little land in Friday Harbor, on which to build a winter place, high up on a secluded knoll where the deer and bunnies run wild, among the mossy banks and fern-studded outcroppings, surrounded with tall firs, madronas, and pine. Jim had put paper and pencil in my hand, saying, "Here, Gramma, draw us a house." It wasn't easy and it hadn't been easy to hold a good man down, so when the call of the wild waves once again murmured, he was off again, leaving me to wind up my own cuckoo clock. He flew to Newport News to join the *American Mail* as navigator of this brand new flagship of the company, just out of the shipyards, a cargo-passenger ship of the very latest design with pilot house control, the newest innovation of the American Merchant Marine. She was 600 feet long and 6 or 7 Cindys wide. (The *Cindy* was Fran and Bill's new gillnetter)

The Grabers of California were so eager for the "Waldron Word" that Betty wrote, "Please tell all." Well, the Frenches were not much for publicity and fanfare, but I hoped they wouldn't mind a few words of farewell. Marjorie said that selling their Waldron acres was the hardest decision she ever had to make. However, they needed to make a change for various and sundry reasons, so they sold their Sandy Point property and bought another place on Orcas which was a little less isolated.

Needless to say, their leaving was like losing a vital part of the island itself; Irving's dignity as a man, his subtle humor and helpful neighborliness, and Marjorie's unwavering and sympathetic friendliness. She had also been a competent leave replacement for me in the post office whenever needed. They had lived on the island for over twenty years.

The last glorious days of summer were upon us; the

chirping crickets, ripening fruit, poetic mornings, dynamic evenings, sun's red glow, and ever-changing hues on the quiet waters. Memorable moonlight, that stirred the imagination as the McDonald's old boat, the *Sloppy Sal*, drifted out to meet the night, perhaps choosing a more romantic fate on some far-off shore rather than submit to the flames which had been planned for her demise.

A passing steamer and the high tide conspired to avenge the derelict's displacement by *Zorka*, the new and more favored aluminum craft, lifting and tossing the *Sloppy Sal* far up the beach, filling her cylinders with sand and Mac's heart with sadness.

Could it have been an omen, the "Waldron Word" in the obituary section? Could the spring be running dry, cables corroding or spark plugs needing changing? Were we really becoming a dead island with thistles and briars taking over, where once fat cattle used to roam? Was it just a seasonal slump, this lowest ebb in time with no young families coming to replace the old and no children to rehabilitate the school?

We hoped it was only history repeating itself and that in a few years it would be fruitful again. We had little Sophie Scruton making strides; she was only five months old but already she had outgrown her first cradle and was exploring her mother's world on sturdy little limbs with an engaging smile.

I remember when almost the same conditions existed on the island and it was June Burn who had advertised for a teacher with a family, offering ten acres of land as inducement to teach on the island. June was like that, always doing the unexpected and dramatic; she had a zest for exploring life, affecting life, and exploiting nature's gifts.

June and Farrar had finally found their Shangri-La, which turned out to be an ordinary boy's home town in Van Buren, Arkansas, which was Farrar's birthplace. June's vibrant and wandering spirit at last found its resting place there in the fall of '69.

June had been a crusader for sight without glasses, health and nutrition, and gardening without chemicals. She was as restless and changeable as the wind, she could endear or reject a person in the same breath, but on these subjects she had been constant. Now she is a legend among the islands and the glow of her vibrant personality will linger on.

Phil's Swiss Chalet, the High Rise as some called it, with its balconies, balustrades, and many bathrooms, had its roof on by Christmas. All it needed now was a few Alps behind it and a goat or two. In all seriousness, it is a monumental product of engineering and structural skill.

The island had settled back into a profound silence again after the happy hordes of Waldron families swooped down from the skies for a few days of communal festivities. News is scarce but if you would like to draw up a log and sit awhile I will share with you an experience I had one day in Friday Harbor.

Once upon a time there was a garden just off Main Street where the most beautiful flowers grew and in it was a little pool where the lily pads flourished. It was like an oasis in the desert, a beauty spot enjoyed by the whole town. I came often to this low-walled shrine to do homage to the gods of color, grace, and form, where dainty daffodils, tulips, and iris abounded in their season; delphiniums, painted daisies, and poppies in profusion; larkspur, lilies, and pungent bright chrysanthemums to delight the eye while the birds and bees were busy in the banana trees.

Then one day that old snake in the grass, progress, came prowling around and coveted this little Garden of Eden. Marge Guard had invited me to a dig-in to identify some plants that were being given away for the taking. I was quite excited but when I learned of the location of the operation I was utterly dismayed. I felt like an intruder on this hallowed earth, so rich in good humus, worked with tender loving care by Lyman Phifer, owner and creator of this spot. I felt a great deal of sympathy for him for the choice must have been a weighty one, to make way for the new building for the telephone company. I felt sort of guilty, caught in the act, so to speak, for we were attracting more attention by our digging than the Girl Scouts' bake sale across the street.

I didn't know Mr. Phifer very well, but I remember many years back when he had to fine me a hundred dollars for aiding and abetting in a misdemeanor. I had been caught with the goods. He just walked up and knocked on my door and asked if he could look into my refrigerator, and being an obliging and honest soul I opened up. My face must have been as red as that out-of-season venison that had found its way in there. Lyman was an enigma to many with his sober countenance, but I am sure, under it all, there was a heart of gold.

Here today and gone tomorrow, that was my Jim. The *American Mail* had been tied up because of a long-shoremen's strike, giving him extra time at home. The fun was soon over and he was headed back to the Orient. Jim liked the music of the waves. Included in his last cargo were five thousand tons of artificial flowers from Hong Kong. It was hard to visualize that many, but it sure ought to have made a lot of flower people happy.

After seeing Jim off, I came back from the mainland with these observations—Mama duck and eight little ducklings jay-waddling across the freeway while the passengers on the bus held their breath; they made it! Seattle policemen with daffodils tied to their billy sticks during a peace rally.

It was a fun day for all involved when Thelma Swan, census enumerator from Orcas, was given the grand tour. She was met at the plane by one of the local taxi trucks and first stopped at the cemetery to admire the two immense and beautiful dogwood trees, then at their peak of bloom. Next they stopped at the schoolhouse grounds to see the gracefully spreading maple tree, then on down to

Margaret Severson's place with its brightly painted wagon-wheel gates and ancient buggy.

There were pebbled pathways to the Burn's, pretty little lady slippers in the moss, and the fragrant balm of Gilead buds unfolding their greenery. We went down a winding roadway to Ralph's, where we met his sister, Gertrude Collins, and back over boulders and butts when we ran into a rail fence, and on down to Sandy Point to see George Buzzelle, the caretaker, who told us of having left his gate open and how the sheep had eaten off his three-inch peas.

"A delightful couple," Thelma said of the McDonalds, who presented her with a nosegay of wallflowers. We had lunch with sister Geva, who was visiting me, and a few pleasantries with Roy Bucknell. From our senior citizen, Fred McNaught, "Senseless, too many questions." At some of the houses the key word seemed to be "Vacant." A few provided incomplete data, but the rest of us stood up to be counted.

It was a memorable May and as we journeyed into June the postal social hour was spent talking of many things—the merits of wild blackberries, salal, Oregon grape, thimble, and salmon berries for making jams and jelly; the merits and un-merits of the new modern gas-powered mowers. For Margaret, who has the magic touch, they would run like a charm; but I'd have to coax it, cool it, and ignore it; then trying a little tenderness, I'd clean out the filter and away it would go. I could remember when the cows and sheep did all the mowing.

Heard tell there had been an invasion on the island with the Army taking over when their helicopter landed on the North Shore beachhead. Mac had complained that they landed right in the middle of his poppy patch. When the Buceys saw Jimmy surrounded by soldiers they thought, "Oh, oh, there goes our mechanic." But Jimmy was just leading them in operation clam dig and by the time they left they believed he had converted them all to the good earth and some movement for peace. The army men did their exercising, which had been the purpose of their visit.

Sailors beware! These Sound waters are not all as serene as they seem, and no matter how large and fancy the cruiser, a man and his mate do not necessarily mariners make, without a little knowledge of the whims of the wind and turn of the tide. A couple of Canadians came drifting down, calling, "Halloa, out there, where are we? We are lost and our tank registers empty." I offered to give them some gas, but it couldn't have fueled them to Gull Rock, and they didn't seem to know how to tie up. I gave them instructions on how to navigate to Roche Harbor; they said they had a chart, but the last I saw of them the tide was carrying them down to Friday Harbor.

Of course, there are many capable couples. Take the gallant gillnet gal, Fran Chevalier; she knows a thing or two about buoys and boats. When Bill left for Bristol Bay he had every confidence in her that she could manage the *Cindy* and sail the crew up to Waldron from Friday Harbor. I was in the cabin chewing my nails while Fran was up on the flying bridge. When we reached the foot of the airfield on the beach, she hove to, lowered the lifeboat, and let me off to get the Ford Bronco that I had left parked there. During the time it took me to drive to North Beach, Fran had reached the buoy with her five little M's, Marilyn (Cindy), Matt, Marty, Mitchell and the dog Misty. She unloaded all the gear and groceries into the rowboat when she heard a big splash. It was Marty. He had fallen overboard. No one panicked as he came up grinning—Fran just kept encouraging him to keep swimming (he was only eight), and the water was deep. He dog-paddled 'til she fished him out of the water, and he said, shivering and shaking, that it was just like dishwater. What pluck and what a boy he was, my grandson. If I had been there at the time I would have had hysterics.

There was a bit of furor on the island because of the

possibilities of a forced annexation of our school district. We had a meeting of a sort to acquaint people with the law as it was presented to Tony Scruton, Clerk of the Board, and the advisability of procuring professional help. According to the old-timers, the land upon which the school now stood was donated to the island and the building erected by long hours of community labor and love, so we felt it rightfully belonged to the island. Who was to know how the wind would blow in a few years. Even though we were presently limited to two, babies seemed to be the fashion again.

Everywhere there was change; now we had padlocks on the post office (required), dust, doubt, discrimination, and ugly notices. "No Smoking, Please," "Keep Waldron Green," and, "No Dogs Allowed, Keep Waldron Serene." (It was a doggone shame; no meeting house for all those visiting canines) As the people population grew, so grew man's best friends. Wow!

With my approaching retirement as postmaster there had been talk of discontinuing service to the island, as such, and replacing it with a rural route, without an appointed postmaster, with exchange of mail services at the airport. This, of course, had caused considerable concern, but when Postal Services Officer Lyle Simons visited the island to meet the people and interview Anna Jo Scruton, who was to be the temporary officer-in-charge, he seemed to be impressed, having had no idea of the size of our summer population. So for the time being business went on as usual while the Post Office Department studied the situation.

The day previous to my retirement was such a beautiful one to begin with: sunny skies, fluffy white clouds, air fresh and invigorating, a perfect day for a walk on the beach and quiet roads. I needed to see Jimmy Bucknell as the "Bronco" was ailing (I used to call it "Buttercup"—it had been such a pretty yellow), so I started off across the old Allen place to the familiar trail to the beach, passing

Ralph's cabin and the Magraw's 'til I came to the Ludwig's, stopping a while to visit with Mildred, with whom I had a spot of tea and refreshment, then continued on my way to Carol and Jim's place on North Beach.

It was mid-afternoon when I started home, going down Charlie's Road. I decided to take a short cut through the old Adrian acres. I reached the cabin where Dote Allen and her first husband lived many years ago. Things were pretty well grown up but there were a few sheep trails, and starting down one which seemed familiar, I was suddenly confronted by a large sheep which just stood there until I cried, "Baa-aa-a," and it took off. That was when I made a wrong decision; if I had followed the sheep I wouldn't have had a tale to tell. Heading for the westering sun I took a different trail, that led to nowhere but deep woods and underbrush; the wild blackberries grew in profusion and I had eaten a few handfuls, but I was not looking for berries; my only concern was to get out of my dilemma before dark.

I contemplated staying for the night on some mossy tree trunk or fir needle nook, but I abandoned the idea when I heard the hoot of an owl. A little breeze had sprung up in the tree tops causing some creaky old snags to eerily rub against each other. So I fought on through the thistles and underbrush while tenacious tendrils and blackberry thorns tore at my face and clothing.

When I at last saw the rosy afterglow reflected on the tip of Point Disney, I said a little prayer of thanks, the sight was so sweet. Although I had an almost impenetrable barbed wire fence covered with thorny briars, and one more swamp to cross, I managed to reach Mr. Gumina's cabin, that the Gordons had built, and asked for a drink of water. I was exhausted and somewhat incoherent. The McKinleys had been kind but they took me for a tramp, I was so disheveled and dirty. They asked me where my camp was, or my boat. After they heard my story and were convinced that I was a bona fide and respected citizen, they walked me the rest of the way home.

The following day there was the changing of the guard at the post office. While Inspector M.C. Nelson was making the transfer, people gathered, bringing coffee and refreshments, and I was presented with a scroll, tied with yellow ribbon, by little Sophie Scruton. It was a loving tribute from all my friends and patrons, a very touching scene. Pictures were taken of Anna Jo with one hand on the postal bible (PL & B's) with right hand raised in the solemnity of the occasion as she was sworn in as our new handler of the mails. In a more relaxed atmosphere, congratulations were in order for all concerned and there was champagne for those who wished it.

Reporting is like going to sea, it gets in one's blood. So habit dictated that I bring the Island Word. I couldn't sing my swan song without writing about the delightful party given for me by our most gracious host and hostess, Chuck and Mildred Ludwig. Literally, they gave me the red carpet, and as Mildred unrolled it I jauntily sashayed down the aisle, as they knew I would, throwing kisses to all my friends, young and old, new and familiar, who gathered to express their appreciation of the twenty years' entrustment of their most precious commodity, the mail.

There were a few statistics presented by Lizanne Magraw: January 1970 had been the 92nd anniversary of the Waldron Post Office; George Dingham, its first postmaster, served for three years; Annie Fernette served in that capacity for thirty-five years, and I had been the thirteenth.

The funniest and perhaps the most embarrassing incident of my years was when I had sung in a high soprano voice, "Who's that knocking at my door?" when a postal inspector came to call. I refrained from singing the last verse, "When will I see you again, said the fair young maiden."

The one and only claim I had paid was for some rifled kosher sausage that I like to refer to as the "Case of the Missing Link."

I was so excited I was too jittery to hold the pottery that was given to me by my island friends, a handsome, large-sized salad bowl by Mideke of Bellingham and a precious picture, a study in black and white gulls on the wing drawn by our very own artist, Paul Glenn.

Another social event of no mean proportions came one afternoon at the Seltzer's, whose hospitality by then needed no introduction. People had been invited to meet, greet, and talk to Phil Wallis and his wife, Gail, from the San Francisco chapter of the Nature Conservancy, a young organization founded in 1951 by those interested in the preservation of our forests, natural birds, and wildlife sanctuaries, and such, to save them from the ever en-croaching bulldozer and pollutionists. The Wallises were just looking the situation over in the San Juans, hoping to find some kindred spirits, a few philanthropists, land and money donors.

I had to leave early; retirement was not all sitting in a rocking chair collecting Social Security and pensions. First you have to prove that you were born, tracking down birth certificates or baptismal papers; tear up the boards if necessary—just find them! Fortunately, just as I was about to wield the crowbar, I spotted a likely looking receptacle under the eaves, and there they were. Just for the fun of it, I stripped the piano to its ivories, removed layers and layers of stain which had been covering up the natural grain and beauty of walnut, put on a new finish, and only had two screws left over. Maybe I would get to the rocker later.

Chapter Twenty
Going Ashore
1971-1976

Jim could never really be separated from the sea, but his career of 47 years aboard deep sea sailing vessels came to an end when he retired in December, 1971.

We built and furnished our crow's nest in Friday Harbor and Jim bought a small cruiser, planked hull and square stern, that had seen better days, but it gave him something to tinker with on the waterfront. We went back to the scrubbing and scraping, painting and varnishing. We still had the *Java Jim* for fast trips, but to Jim, a boat was not a boat unless it had a pilot house, a galley, and a couple of bunks.

Phil retired to the island in 1972. His house was completed and he was happy and content among all his growing things, making a vegetable garden and preparing ground for more fruit trees and ornamentals. These were the supreme moments which he had been working toward, when his house would overflow with family and guests, showing them the mountain and the now billion dollar view, and his magnificent redwood trees (Sequoia gigantea), chestnuts, and dogwood, and his system of ponds and waterworks. In the summertime Jim and I shuttled back and forth to the island, sharing in all the good times.

We traveled to California for a reunion of my five sisters and one remaining brother, and saw the Redwoods and ocean surf. We crossed the North Cascades into Utah, Montana, and South Dakota to visit for the first time Jim's brother, Joe, and his wife, Dorothy, and young son, Jim. We returned by way of the Black Hills and the Badlands, seeing the famous Rushmore carvings and the geysers in

Yellowstone Park. We went the coast route all the way to Los Angeles to see Jim's sister, Stella, who was now retired from teaching. From there we drove to Oroville, and we continued north along the Feather River, where my father used to pan for gold. We stopped at Yosemite, we saw Crater Lake, the Lava Beds and The Dalles in Oregon.

Our last journey together took us to Victoria, B.C., and the fabulous Butchart Gardens, over the Canadian Rockies to Banff and Lake Louise. Then on across the country for a second visit to South Dakota, coming back through Wyoming, seeing more of the wonders of nature, the Grand Tetons, whose magnificence defies description. But the memory of all the places we saw is reflected in that inner eye, tucked away to bring to mind at a moment's bidding. At such times I believe that memory is one of our most amazing gifts.

Jim's final voyage was a stormy one; he was pitched and tossed on the sea of heart surgery and post-operative indignities, until his ship of life foundered. On May 18, 1976, he abandoned ship for more peaceful shores, and his parting words were, "Everything is going to be all right. I love you, darling." We had said our goodbyes so many times before, but this one was our last farewell; I knew this time he was going to meet his master. I said goodbye to my sailorman. He is at peace now, in the San Juan County Cemetery.

A church friend has written the following words of tribute in his memory:

To Captain James Lovering by Frances M. Seels

How fortunate we were to have known him.
A man of few words was the Captain,
And his smile was something to see.
A man of God was the Captain,
A friend to "just folks" like me.

Beloved husband and father—the Captain,
And a grandfather, wise as could be.
His love will remain with us always,
As sure as there's salt in the sea.

Epilogue
This Is My Song

Since my retirement from Waldron there have been many changes. The population has grown considerably with people of new and different life styles. The post office business is carried on as usual in our log cabin building down by the dock. Anna Jo Scruton served as postmaster for four years, followed by Roy Bucknell, Oliver Wilgress, and currently Chris Weaver.

After many years of successful flying of the mails by Island Mail, Inc., the Post Office Department finally accepted aircraft as a fact of life in the San Juans and is now letting its contract out for four-year periods. Island Mail, Inc., owned the contract which ended in 1982. However, since the Waldron Community Comprehensive Plan came into being, direct airplane service to Waldron came to an abrupt halt.

Bill Carlson, the owner of the airfield, wanted to divide some of his property into lots for sale to flyers and their families, which he planned to call *Waldronair*. The planners turned thumbs down on his project, declaring it not compatible with the serenity of the island because of its probable noise, pollution, and possible danger. Subsequently, Mr. Carlson closed his airfield to all aircraft. Later he made a concession to allow San Juan Airlines to land in an emergency or for an occasional charter.

So mail and freight are now handled by boat again. Tony Scruton came to the rescue. He is following almost the same route as the island's first postmaster over a century ago, taking the mail across President Channel to West Beach on Orcas in the *Puffin*, a 27-foot wooden double-ender, powered by an inboard diesel motor.

While there is a recession in air service, the school goes booming ahead. The district was annexed to Orcas Island in 1970 and the school re-opened in the fall of 1972 with Mary Weaver presiding as teacher until her retirement in 1978. During this time a handsome new addition was built onto the existing building to serve as library. The materials and some labor were paid for by the district, but, as of yore, there were many willing hands donating time and talents to its completion.

Subsequently, there was projected a preliminary budget for the coming school year of $40,000 with state matching funds. It sounds fantastic! Of this amount, $8,000 was earmarked for an asphalt playground with improvements to the existing equipment. An enrollment of twenty-two pupils was anticipated and the Board feels there will soon be a need for two full-time teachers and two part-time aides. It almost staggers my mind when I think of those days past.

It is gratifying to know that some facets of the island will remain the same, and that the Nature Conservancy has been successful in raising the necessary funds to purchase land to preserve parts of the island in its natural state. Mr. Guminas was as good as his word and sold some 250 acres for the cause. This includes some swampy land, a most delightful spot which has always been a wild fowl sanctuary.

Margaret Severson, the last of the real pioneers of Waldron and in her 92nd year, is still cultivating her mother's original acres to which she has added many lovely trees. In 1978, she was awarded a plaque and holds the loving cup given by the San Juan Pioneer Association for being the oldest pioneer for the year.

Jim's brother, Phil, another avid tree planter, is in his late eighties and is still beautifying his place with shrubs and rose bushes. Among his many other chores he never forgets to raise and lower the American flag, a tradition he believes in and was taught as a boy. I asked him why he planted so many fruit trees and he replied, "In my time I have enjoyed so much fruit from the labors of those gone before me that I want to leave something for someone else to enjoy." His words brought to mind some verses I noticed in a Bible study series by Dr. William Barclay, world-renowned New Testament interpreter. I quote from his Daily Study Bible series *The Gospel of St. Mark* published by the St. Andrew Press:

In youth, because I could not be a singer
I did not even try to write a song;
I set no little trees along the roadside
For I knew their growth would take so long.
But now from wisdom that the years have brought me
I know it might be a blessed thing,
To plant a tree for someone else to water,
Or make a song for someone else to sing.

So this is my song, this is my tree, and this is my book for someone else to read. I count my blessings as I tend my flowers which I give to the altar of St. David's Church. Father Leche calls it my *Ministry of Flowers*. Now I can be content to watch the little birds who gather 'round my feeder; they sing me their lullaby. I can be content to watch the eagles soaring high overhead; I sing my own song.

Printed in the United States
128756LV00001B/133-498/P

9 780981 809236